AF522564

The Corpse Collector

The Corpse Collector

A True Story

Vinu P and Niyas Kareem

Translated from the Malayalam by
Ministhy S.

JUGGERNAUT BOOKS
C-I-128, First Floor, Sangam Vihar, Near Holi Chowk,
New Delhi 110080, India

First published by Juggernaut Books 2026
Originally published in the Malayalam as *Maranakkoottu* by
Mathrubhumi Books 2024

Images Courtesy: G. Harikrishnan

10 9 8 7 6 5 4 3 2 1

P-ISBN: 9789353455217
E-ISBN: 9789353458973

Typeset in Adobe Caslon Pro by R. Ajith Kumar, Noida

Printed at Thomson Press India Ltd

To Vinu,
who drew me into a life stranger than
any imagined tale;

To his Masters,
who shaped his path and taught him
how to set aside one's ego;

And to the Kerala Police,
who stood by him firmly when others moved away.

Janthukkal bhakshichu kashtichu pokilam
Vendhu veneeray chamanju poyidilam
Manninnu keezhay krimikalay pokilam
Nannalla deham nimittam mahamoham!

– EZHUTHACCHAN, renowned as the Father of Malayalam literature

[Eaten and excreted by animals
Burnt to cinders and ashes
Rendered as maggots under the earth,
The body – not good, the hubris stirred by that grand delusion!]

Contents

Preface

Here Stands the Companion of Death

The path ended abruptly. A vast yard, ridden with weeds and wilderness, lay ahead. One solitary house stood in the middle. When I rang the bell, a man stepped out. The man I was looking for. All by himself. The hero of the book I wanted to write. I was there to ask his permission to write his story. There were remnants of a *kalabha kuri* (sacred paste that is applied to one's forehead) on his face.

When I extended my hand after introducing myself, he stopped me: 'Please Sir, don't touch me! I just returned from work.'

He walked towards the ambulance parked in the courtyard. He used it as a hearse van to transport the dead. When I told Vinu that I wanted to record his memoirs, he put forth just one condition. 'You can write whatever you wish about me. But not a single word should degrade a corpse or the Kerala Police.'

Lowering his voice, he continued: 'Let us move away from here. My parents are there in the house. If they see me sharing my story with you, they will get upset. Except my wife, nobody supports my work.'

In the twilight, as the bats came to life, I accompanied Vinu to a nearby railway track. We perched on the iron rails, next to a swamp which was a dumping ground for garbage. Vinu lit a *beedi*.

The man who sat near me, with his face blazing, was someone ostracized by society because of his chosen work; not due to caste, religion or the colour of his skin. His chosen profession – something he had elected to do freely, of his own will – was to gather the remains of those who had met untimely deaths. Society had given him, a man with a bottomless reservoir of compassion, a cruel, mocking nickname: '*Shavamvari*' or 'Corpse Collector'.

Incessantly puffing away, Vinu started speaking tremulously. 'I am not used to talking to strangers. Usually nobody ever wants to talk to me.'

Suddenly, he stopped. Vinu's nostrils flared alertly. 'Sir, I catch a smell. Do you get a whiff too?'

I tried to sniff. There was an overpowering stench of the dumping site; I could not sense any other odour.

'A snake –' Before Vinu could finish, a huge snake slithered from beneath the shrubs and crossed the railway tracks. Vinu grinned.

With such a remarkable sensitivity to smells, how could this man tolerate rotting corpses? I had no answer. In the days, weeks and months that followed, after many deep conversations, I discovered that Vinu was an enigma. A question without an answer.

I often found myself speechless as he narrated the story of his life – an existence which ran on a parallel track, separate, apart from, mainstream society. While reading the works of writers like Jeyamohan, Sharankumar Limbale or Omprakash Valmiki, we often encounter the marginalized lives of human beings like Vinu. One wonders: 'Can there be people like him in today's world?'

It can sound unbelievable that in such an enlightened state like Kerala, society treats a human being who does the unavoidable, essential work of removing rotting cadavers like a rabid dog, driving him away with horror and loathing.

Some truths are heartrending. As Benyamin wrote in *Aadujeevitham* (*Goat Days*): 'All the lives which we have never lived appear as fables.'

Perhaps, Vinu's life is one of the truest fables of our times.

One day, after our discussions, I asked Vinu: 'When will you be free tomorrow?'

His answer: 'Sir, every day I pray that nobody calls me for work. My job is to collect the dead bodies of those who have met horrible endings. Let no one demand my presence, tomorrow or any day. Wherever I go, I witness shattered homes.'

Where will you find a human being like Vinu? Someone who prays that nobody should call him for work, even as he dedicates his body and soul to his profession?

I am offering Vinu's life to the readers in his own words.

Niyas Kareem

1

On the Cliff of Hope

This incident happened a decade ago.

A motorbike was discovered under suspicious circumstances in a deserted hilly area, near the highway route connecting Munnar and Kanthalloor. A few workers of the neighbouring resorts had noticed the bike. Usually, only visitors to the resorts came that way. The bike was parked on top of a huge boulder. A deadly gorge, almost 150 ft deep, loomed beneath. It was only natural that the locals called the cops.

During the preliminary investigations, some facts were ascertained. The bike rider was not alone. Perhaps it was a couple. Either they had met with an accident or died by suicide. Since there were no signs of foul play or accident, it was concluded that the couple had chosen to jump off the rock.

It was highly risky to explore the ravine. To add to the woes, there was a formidable, thick mist. One could hardly see the face of the man standing a short distance away. What could the police do under such circumstances?

Dusk arrived, but there was no information available of the missing couple. The police decided to pitch camp temporarily at the summit. They were also trying to get in touch with men in the whereabouts who dealt with dead bodies. There was an old man in that region who used to undertake such tasks. There was no way that he would slither down the gorge and retrieve the corpses. Usually, people got stone drunk before attempting such feats. Of course, that was totally ruled out in this particular case. Nobody in their right senses would take such a huge risk. They sought help from neighbouring districts. That is how the Munnar Police got to know about the man in Aluva.

A police jeep from Munnar halted in front of my house at midnight. In two hours, I was seated in the vehicle which was speeding to the high range.

I was taken straight to the spot of the tragedy. It was half past five in the morning. Bone-chilling cold wrapped around the desolate heights. The preparations began. Two vehicles of the fire force stood ready, fully equipped with iron wire ropes, crane and nets. The revenue divisional officer who held magisterial powers, superintendent of the fire force and police surgeon were present. There was a posse of police, local politicians and villagers. Many journalists from print and TV channels clamoured around. An ambulance and medical team were on standby, in case, the missing couple was found alive.

It was eleven in the morning when all arrangements were completed. I puffed a beedi to keep away the cold. My teeth chattered in that bitter chill. One was not used to such a hostile climate. I was clad in a heavy-duty jacket made of flame-retardant material used by the fire force, with multiple pockets and secure closures, and hooked up to a safety belt. They had armed me with a whistle, sacks and a wireless set. Whether the wireless would work in the deep ravine was something I had no clue about. The whistle was meant to alert everyone on discovering the dead bodies or when facing any danger. The sacks were for bringing up the corpses.

I was working in a high range area (elevated hilly land) for the first time in my life. If the iron wire rope broke, I would be shattered to smithereens. Though my life was at stake, I did not feel any fear. There were police and fire force officers ready to help me. Besides, I had a clear goal in front. There were loving hearts waiting far away for these missing persons, who fell knowingly or unknowingly in the gorge.

After tying the iron rope to the crane, they started slowly lowering me into the ravine. After a little while, when I gazed upwards, I could see nothing! There was no glimpse of the crane or anybody around. Only a heavy mist, that stubbornly refused to leave the surroundings. The cold became biting as I descended. I could hear both my chattering teeth and my heartbeats.

In darkness, once your eyes get used to it, a faint glimmer appears. I could make out some silhouettes in that hazy white mist around me. First, the jagged edges of rocks. Then it became a muddle of slopes with waving grass. *What the hell is this?* I felt as if sinking deep into a surreal, feverish dream.

When I reached almost 60 ft down, I noticed

blood on the rock nearby. I blew the whistle, signalling my finding. I started exploring the area. There were layered rocks descending into the abyss. After a detailed search, I saw the girl's body lying some distance away. When I touched the body, it was very cold. All of life's warmth had long seeped away. The death must have occurred a few hours before. I safely wrapped the corpse in a sack and signalled to have it pulled up. I continued my search, since the boy's body was not to be seen anywhere.

When I reached almost a 100 ft down, there was a rocky layer which was vast and ridden with grass. There, after much searching, I found the dead body of the boy. In the powerful impact, his body had splintered into two. Packing the body parts in a sack, I signalled to the officers to pull me up. As I ascended, holding the lifeless body of the strange young man close to my heart, he suddenly felt very dear to me.

A mother was waiting for him somewhere, worried out of her mind, unaware of the tragedy that had befallen her son. I was helpless when it came to saving the young man's life. At least I could retrieve his body so that his loved ones could take a last look.

That satisfaction became the greatest reward in the dangerous game of gambling with my own life.

The dead bodies were shifted to the Munnar Government Hospital, and later to the Kottayam Medical College for post-mortem formalities. Everybody – the officers, politicians and villagers – appreciated me for the successful accomplishment of that perilous assignment. I saw affection and admiration in many eyes. I remembered myself as a fifteen-year-old boy, all those years before, who stared awestruck at the men who dived into the Periyar River, searching for a corpse.

While that image was brimming over in my eyes, many villagers came forward to chat. They wished to know my name and where I hailed from. Many were caught by surprise that I had travelled from Aluva to Munnar to recover the dead bodies. Some generously tucked money into my pocket. The police officers paid me handsomely. They also gave me good food. Though I had retrieved more than 1,500 corpses till then, none was more challenging than the Munnar suicide case.

I was standing on top of a mountain peak, so far away from home, overwhelmed by the love and affection of a large crowd. For the natives, the place might be an infernal 'suicide point'. But it was a cliff of hope for me. Never in my life had I stood with my spine erect, at such a height, surrounded by light and openness. My yesterdays were fraught with memories of hiding like a rat in the pits of darkness.

Even if the afternoon sun of the present day shines very bright, one cannot forget the darkness of the past's withered nights. My memories started blazing a trail, amid the day's din.

2

Nest of Angels

Acchan, my father, walked ahead as always. Though there was no beedi peeking from his lips, the confidence of a good smoke gleamed like moonlight on his face. When they crossed the gate, Amma, my mother, ran forward, clutching her swollen stomach. She was nervous about seeking refuge at an unfamiliar place.

The charming compound was lush with trees. When she stepped into the shade, Amma's anxiety abated a bit. Even then, she clutched Acchan's hand tightly. It was not a usual practice, but she still held on to his hand. As they made their way through the neat gravel path, they read the Biblical quotation painted on the wall of a building on the right: '*Fear not, for I am with you.*'

The missionary sisters of the convent welcomed my mother with the warmth of inviting a daughter home for childbirth. She was allotted a decent room. Acchan left to go to work with the relief of having ensured the safety of his pregnant wife. He worked in the convent as a washerman and also helped with the ironing.

My parents had lived in Aluva, a place called Kodikuthumala, before I was born. Every morning, my father would go for work to the convent at Perumbavoor. Amma would be all alone until he returned at night. Acchan became worried as I started growing in her womb. Later, when the delivery was due, he decided to move my mother to the convent. He was determined that no crease should deform the fabric of his family.

The convent had its own dispensary. A few days after my mother shifted there, she gave birth to me. Forty years ago, to be precise. There were many mothers, not just one, to look after me. Pregnant cats seek a home when they are due to give birth to a litter; and there are those who look at the mother cat and her kittens with compassion. Perhaps a similar sentiment might have been evoked in the nuns on sighting my mother and me. Anyway, I was fortunate to have been born in a heaven, where angels with white wings hovered around lovingly. I must have smiled delightedly on seeing their angelic faces. Though the angels left my life soon after, whenever I see missionary sisters, I recollect the stories that Amma narrated to me. My heart fills with inexpressible love and gratitude at those moments.

❧

Acchan's name is Purushottaman; he hails from Aluva. Amma's name is Ambika; her land is North Paravoor. My father's family had been the washermen of the Aluva royal palace for almost eight generations. His family house stood on the land given by the palace. Acchan smoked beedis and cigarettes. But he never touched liquor. He has always been very popular with the villagers.

My parents had fallen in love, but they hailed from different castes. As was the practice, the man and woman faced social and family boycott. They shifted to a small, rented house. I was their second child; my elder sibling was older than me by fifteen years. I have never been close to him. When he was young, my Chettan, elder brother, was taken away by my maternal grandmother. He grew up with her, at the family house in Paravoor.

My parents returned to their house in Kodikuthumala a few days after my birth. We stayed there for a couple of years. Meanwhile, Amma gave birth to my sister. She died very young, due to *karappan* (acute eczema). After my sister's death, we shifted to Ashokapuram, a neighbourhood within Aluva Municipality, which I identify as being my homeland. When the land acquisition happened for a highway project in the Aluva–Ernakulam route, people were allotted land in Ashokapuram. The compound behind Ashoka company, thus became a colony of settlers. That's where I grew up.

Our colony was the prowling ground of *goonda*s in my childhood. Thugs and quotation teams* also known as contract killers. The place was a headache for the police force. One day, a scuffle broke out in

---

*Quotation team or quotation gang refers to criminal groups in Kerala that offer violent services for a price. They undertake any illegal services, from intimidation to murder for hire, for a fee.

the colony. In the daytime, people would leave their front doors open. A few goondas came rushing inside our home. We were flabbergasted. Acchan, after recovering his composure, asked them firmly to leave his house. But they ignored him. He started abusing them and ordered them to get out. It soon became a brawl and there was some manhandling involved. Acchan lashed out physically. His response became problematic. There was now a target on his back. Eventually, we left the place. I was a toddler then.

We shifted to a decrepit house next to the Chovvara railway gate, almost 5 km away from Aluva town. The house smelt of iron grating against iron. There was a constant odour of the train, and its growls and rumbles echoed around the house. House? It was not a house in reality. Imagine two bamboo poles and a tarpaulin sheet pitched across a septic tank covered with cement blocks. That was our home. My father's family in Chovvara was extremely well off. But due to his inter-caste marriage, they had discarded him totally. One of his relatives, Josettan, offered to give free land for building a house. My father did not accept it. His pride got in the way. We continued to live above the septic tank.

After a few years, we purchased 3 cents near the Ashokapuram ground. (A cent is equivalent to 435.6 sq. ft.) My father built a small thatched house. The land cost ₹2,000 in those days. The problems with the local goondas were old stories now.

After quitting his job at the convent, my father worked in many different places. Finally, he ended up at Johnettan's shop. My father and his friend John, whom we called Johnettan, started a partnership ironing business. 'Partnership ironing shop' might sound hilarious to many ears. Our family survived because of that shop.

I was admitted to Mandiram School at Ayyappankavu – near the Ayyappa temple, a short distance from Ernakulam – for my first standard. Amma had started selling fish by then. She could not manage the household merely on my father's earnings. My mother would set off from home early in the morning, with me in tow. First, she would prepare the mid-day meal at my school – rice gruel and boiled green grams. That was a source of extra income for her. Afterwards, she would go off to sell fish. She had loyal purchasers who were rich. By evening, she would be back to pick me up from school and we would go home together. The first standard education happened in that way.

By the second year, Amma could not travel daily to Ernakulam. She shifted her fishmongering job to Aluva. I joined Ashoka School, near our house. After a few months, I was taken out and admitted to St Mary's. It was located in front of my father's ironing shop. I was once again enrolled in the first standard. I was very young and first standard was appropriate for my age. Amma had lugged me all the way to school at Ernakulam, only because there was no childcare available.

My father had sought refuge at the convent before I was born. Amma sought refuge at the Mandiram School when I was a little child. For me, life often became an incessant search for refuge.

3

The Friend Who Seized My Jugular

My school days truly began at St Mary's. They say that good things usually come after a period of waiting. St Mary's is one of the oldest schools in Aluva. A gigantic building bang in the middle of the town! The movie theatre, bus stand, railway station, shopping complex, girls' school and bar are all close by. The students of St Mary's were known for participating in every strike and fracas, stoning public buses, smoking cigarettes and *ganja*, drinking, and everything illicit you can imagine under the sun. These things were considered 'heroic' in those days! My family's only solace was that my father's ironing shop was located opposite the school. Every teacher was known to Acchan. They believed that his eagle eyes would always be on me. Until tenth standard, I did not cause much trouble to anyone.

In the morning, my parents and I would start from home together. My father would drop me at school. After school, I would race to his shop. Suma Chechi, in the shop, was affectionate towards me. Amma would return after selling fish and take me home with her.

My little world consisted of my friends, home and school. These were my best years, during which I unapologetically relished life to the hilt! There were no fences around houses in those days. Every door was open to all. One could enter any place, climb any tree, pluck guavas and rose apples. Everyone seemed equal. The women would sit in someone's yard and make brooms from *eerkil*, the central spine of the coconut leaves. The kids would frolic together.

As time passed, fences started appearing. Walls were erected. Religion stepped in. So did faith and rituals. Whatever was open, shut forever. In the past, even though there were many religions and customs, nobody nurtured hatred and enmity in their minds. A human being was seen as a human being.

I was very bad at studies. I wonder how I learnt my lessons from the first standard till the tenth. Failure was a recurring phenomenon. I failed in fifth and seventh standards. Actually, I was more interested in chess than classes. Wherever I could – in the temple grounds, near the banyan tree, in the playground or in friends' houses – I would play chess. I struggled with reading. My policy was 'play and enjoy'.

There were many reasons why my parents enrolled me at St Mary's. They did not have to pay any fees, since it was a government-aided school. A mid-day meal was available. After a light breakfast at home, nobody bothered about my hunger till night-time. I found a way to escape studies. I began helping out with the preparation of the school's mid-day meal: buying the groceries and serving the food. I took over as the main helper during occasions like Onam and Vishu, doling out *kanji* and *payar* (rice gruel and boiled green grams) to the students. This job became my main focus from the sixth standard onwards. To be frank, I went to school to play and serve the mid-day meal.

There were four senior students who helped the woman who prepared the mid day meal. I would stick around with them – addressing each as chettan – and join in cleaning plates, cooking food and doing sundry work. The rest of the students looked at me with awe!

Acchan would give me some pocket money regularly. I spent it on buying sweets for my mentors. They were smart guys who participated in strikes. Everyone was scared of them. To give you an idea of their notoriety: they would uproot every wooden stake of the classroom windows and use it for fights and scuffles! I preened around, having befriended them. Somehow, I managed to reach the ninth standard. The teachers found it a blessing that I spent most of my time outside the classroom.

What was the rest of my school life like? I had two friends in school: Jeemon and Anas. I suffered from breathing problems. Whenever the sickness struck, my friends would accompany me home. We would prowl around the PWD Office near the school, in the heart of Aluva town, and pluck sweet cat eye fruit, with fragrant flowers resembling cat fur, to our heart's content. Cat eye fruit, or *thodali pazham*, is also called wild jujube fruit. Black when ripe, it has a sweet and slightly acidic taste.

We would spit out the seeds as if firing a cannon! Wandering like a scamp and collecting the attractive pictures of birds, animals and vehicles pasted on top of matchboxes became my main hobbies at that point of time.

I disliked school so much that I would pray that I should fall badly ill. Then they would let me go home from school, wouldn't they? Someone told me that if one tucked crushed onion under the armpit and ran around, one would fall woefully sick! I would try wetting my head under a tap hoping to fall ill. No fever ever touched me though I tempted fate often. I preferred to stay out of class, since I would get beaten up by the teacher who would cane me during math class. I had no clue about the subject. Numbers simply refused to enter my head. When I wistfully gazed out of the window, I would see my heroes, the seniors who prepared mid-day meals, astride the school walls. I would slip outside and join them for games: playing marbles; collecting pictures, stickers, labels.

If you did not attend the class, nobody bothered at all. The teachers preferred the studious ones. The rest of us were worthless in their eyes. No teacher ever bothered to find out why we did not understand the lessons or what problems we faced.

Arun and Ajit were my friends in high school. They were twins who were good students. I used to buy them fluffy cotton sweets to bribe them to do my homework! One day, I saw a tall boy with buck teeth in their company. His name was Mithun. Somehow, I did not like the fellow. I started ignoring Mithun, whenever I met him in school.

One day, as I was serving the rice gruel, Mithun approached me aggressively: 'Why are you so damn cocky?'

'What do you mean? Get lost.' I retorted.

'I see you are sheltering under the seniors. Don't be over smart!'

He kept needling me. 'Why don't you mind your business?'

'What will you do, if I don't?'

Mithun grunted angrily. I deposited the vessel of rice on the ground. Then I grabbed his collar. Mithun seized my jugular. We started rolling in the mud. He tore my clothes. Ajit and Arun came running to intervene. They managed to separate us. 'He is our friend, let him go!' They were yelling at Mithun.

Finally, Mithun let go of me. I was furious with him for a few days. Later, we became fast friends. That is the specialty of school days. Those who caught each other's collars became inseparable pals later. We were in the same class at first. Since Mithun was a bright student, he shifted to better divisions like 'B' and 'A' over a span of time. We losers were always in division 'C'. Among us, those who were comparatively better were seated on the front benches. We were always doomed to be the backbenchers. Since there was no more space to be pushed further back, the teachers allowed us to sit there.

Though we were in different classes, Mithun and I were always together. In fact, I could not bear to be apart from him. His father had a car wash centre near the theatre Zeenat. We would cut classes and go for movies, collect matchbox pictures and play. The front bench of Zeenat Theatre cost ₹5. Mata Theatre, slightly far away, charged ₹10. But, when many started playing truant, the teachers would inform the cops. The police would troop into Zeenat Theatre and identify the truant kids in white and blue uniforms easily enough! The teachers would beat us up properly when we returned. They would demand that we bring our guardians to meet them.

As mentioned earlier, everyone knew my father; most of the teachers got their clothes ironed at his shop. 'We will update him about your latest gimmicks,' they would say. They would then inform Acchan, who in turn, would tell Amma. Acchan was tough, but he avoided corporal punishment. Only once has my father thrashed me. He chased me all the way home, after finding me smoking a cigarette! My mother was ruthless when furious. I would run inside the house and shut all the doors to save myself from her wrath!

I had a big crush on a girl in those days. She was my classmate till the fourth standard. Since I adored her, I would follow her to school every day. Though I had never spoken to the girl, I knew her name and address by heart. I would write a love letter daily and manage to sneak it inside her notebook! The letter would be brimming over with poems and movie songs.

One day, unwittingly, I added my address in the letter. That evening, her parents reached my home. 'We want to see Vinu.'

I stood like a thief caught red-handed.

'Stand straight!' her father said. They had a camera with them. Her father clicked my photograph. 'In case you trouble our daughter from today, the police will catch you!'

I was terrified out of my wits. The mere mention of the word 'police' was enough to scare the living daylights out of any child.

A small poetry collection that I wrote, titled *The Paths I Walked*, was released in my school a few years later. The teachers were very happy with me. A backbencher was writing poems and getting them featured in the school assembly! Perhaps, they were under the impression that I had written about the thorns and briars of life's long journey. In reality, it was about the paths I had walked, while trailing after my sweetheart for many long years! Anyway, I ended up getting a trophy for publishing the book – the lone recognition from a school where I studied for ten years.

I have always had a liking for beautiful lyrics. In

fact, I would jot down the lines of movie songs that I admired, in a notebook. S. Janaki had sang:

Kazhinju poya kalam kattinakkare
Kozhinju poya ragam kadalinakkare,
Ormakale ninneyorthu karayunnu njan
Ninte ormakalil veenudanju pidayunnu njan.

[The hours long gone, are beyond the wind
The love that withered, is beyond the sea,
I am lamenting at my memories…
I lie broken, shuddering in your remembrance.]

Whenever I hear that song, I remember my sweetheart. My heart weeps remembering that beautiful time.

The good times of my life did not last very long.

4

A 'C'-Class Existence

They are omnipresent at night. In the farms, gulleys, rail tracks, banana groves, rubber plantations, pala trees, everywhere ... They can enter any house effortlessly. If you see a movement where the darkness is profuse, be afraid! Some take the guise of a woman wearing a white sari, her feet not touching the ground. Others may be that of a man with hooves of a buffalo, asking you for a box of matches, or even a bat or an amorphous flicker of light ... They can appear in front of us in multifarious ways: Yakshi, Maruta, Arumkola, Chattan, Rakshas. They have many names and forms. As a child, I referred to all those spectres as *pretam* or ghosts.

The stories of ghosts were widespread in those days. The children suffered the most. The spirits of the dead haunted them at night. When we lived near the Chovvara railway gate – between 1990, when I was five, and 1994, when I turned nine – the bloodied remains of those who jumped in front of trains would be scattered around our front yard. Though I had never seen a corpse shattered to smithereens, the dead ones would loiter around me in the form of nightmarish stories. I was a boy spooked by ghost tales from childhood.

There was a man called Kartikeyan who was our neighbour at Ashokapuram. He was an early riser. Kartikeyan Chettan was very friendly towards all. Many students would visit him for tuition lessons. Amma would chat with him while setting off early to sell fish. He passed away when I was studying in the seventh standard. My mother started seeing Kartikeyan's apparition on the road after his demise. She was badly frightened.

In those days, I would paste the insignias of all religions – the Cross, the sign of Om, crescent moon of Allah – on the lintel, jambs and sill of the entrance door of the house. No ghost, belonging to any religion, should trespass into my house! Once night fell, I would not stroll in the yard. I did not dare to step out of the door even to urinate; I preferred to open the window for the task. Despite all my precautions, all those corpses wrapped in white, the ghosts of those who killed themselves under trains, would come marching into my house at night. They would surround my bed. Some lacked limbs, some were decapitated. How could I sleep peaceably then?

My fear of dead bodies began at a young age. Any news of death petrified me. My fertile imagination and the endless ghost stories I had heard, added fuel to the flame. 'Never get out of the house in the afternoon. The devil will bash your head!' 'Be wary of Friday afternoons. If you go near a pala tree, only your nails and teeth shall remain.' 'The Yakshi shall make mincemeat out of you. Beware of the banana groves!'

Snakes never frightened me. I was terrified only of ghosts. My elder brother used to eat snakes. Once, when I visited my mother's family house, I saw him hack off the hood of a *manja chera* (Indian rat snake) and cook its flesh. A snake simply meant good meat for the cooking pot.

There was a girl near my house, allegedly possessed by an evil spirit. Apparently a Yakshi had infested her, as she crossed a pala tree at night. On certain occasions, the girl would loosen her hair and start spouting gibberish. Then she would start howling eerily. Whenever I saw her, I would feel chilled to the bones. I shared her story with my classmates and they regaled me with more. A Tamil woman's spirit had purportedly set up residence inside someone's aunt. Every day, at twilight, she would gather soiled clothes and move to the washing stone in the compound. All the while, the woman, who hardly knew proper Malayalam, would jabber in Tamil!

By the time, I finished ninth standard, I became mature. The niggling fear of ghosts had abated a bit. Then, one day at school, someone said that six people were murdered in a neighbouring house. We used to pluck mangoes from that yard. Later, the incident was referred to as the 'notorious Aluva mass murder case'. One victim was a girl my age. It was the first murder I had encountered in my life.

St Mary's did not have any boundary walls. We could see the house from our classroom. A massive crowd thronged the place. Though I wished to take a look at the victims, I did not have the courage. How could someone scared of ghosts bring himself to look at the dead? I saw a photographer for the first time in my life in the middle of the pandemonium. His name was Tomy and he worked at Photonics Studio. Someone whispered that he was the official police photographer.

Leaving aside the horror and mystery of the murder case, our attention was drawn to the photographer. While he was busy taking photographs, we timidly approached him. 'Chetta, can you please click our photo?'

'Let me finish my work first.'

We went to his side intermittently. 'Chetta, a photo please.'

He would tactfully send us away. As mentioned earlier, the students of St Mary's were infamous those days. At the slightest provocation, we would pelt an offender with stones! But we liked Tomy Chettan. He had such wondrous equipment in his hands! Besides, he was very friendly with the cops. Tomy Chettan became my hero from that day. Tired of our constant cajoling, he tricked us by clicking a photograph without inserting film in his camera.

Namboodiri Sir taught us in the ninth standard. Everybody liked him. He would not abuse, hit or beat any student. Instead, Sir would render kind advice. In those days, the other teachers believed in beating the hell out of us. Many students would tie thick areca leaves – *kamukin pala* – beneath their trousers. But the wily teachers would force the students to remove the protective layers and dole out extra hidings to them! Some kids would wear multiple layers of clothes in terror. It was a troublesome time. Beating at school, thrashing at home. The teacher might stop at three lashes with his cane, but my mother would not stop so easily! She would grab whatever was near her hand and start hitting me. I remember often being chased around the house by my incensed Amma.

Everyone had a nickname at school. Once a moniker was given, it usually stuck forever. The dark-skinned one was mocked cruelly as *Marappatti*, toddy cat or the palm civet with its peculiar black face; and the fair skinned kid was taunted as *Vellappatta*, white cockroach. The flabby boy was mocked as a *Veepakkutti* or bulging barrel; the thin lad was compass. I had protruding teeth at that time. By sheer luck, nobody teased me for that. But when I reached the fourth standard, I got my nickname: *Peppatti*, rabid dog.

I had been bitten by a mad dog that year and the dog had died on the tenth day. I almost lost my left eye in that mauling. I was given fourteen injections near my navel. The doctors managed to save my vision. They had tied me up before administering the shots. The treatment was at Ernakulam General Hospital. I developed breathing trouble afterwards. Even now, I wheeze a lot.

❧

Society looks at the rich and the poor with clear differentiation. This is still the case, despite all claims of progress. I have witnessed how poor people are treated as outcastes everywhere. The same prejudice existed at school between those who were studious and those who struggled with their studies. As mentioned earlier, good students would be allotted front row seats and the teachers would display fawning favouritism. Naturally, these students felt contemptuous towards the backbenchers. In the tenth standard, Jeemon, Anas and I remained on the last bench. We considered the front-benchers as our enemies. We picked up fights with them for the slightest reason.

My heroes, the seniors who were experts at mid-day meal preparations, had left the school by the time I reached the tenth standard. Mithun had shifted to the 'A' division by then. I continued in the 'C' division as usual. The 'A' class consisted of those adored by the teachers and the 'C' was full of losers, abandoned by all.

5

Holding Hands with Death

Some shocking news awaited me at school one day when I was studying in the tenth standard. Two students had drowned in the river! They had gone to take a dip in the river, at a dock named Thadikkakadavu, 10 km away from the school. After some time, we heard that one of the boys had been pulled out safely. Nobody knew anything about the second boy. The teachers would not reveal their names, not wanting to cause further distress to the students. By evening, I heard the most staggering news of my life. The boy who had gone missing in the Periyar River was Mithun!

I felt as if a lightning bolt had struck me. I was blinded by grief. Death, which had frightened me from afar, was standing next to me. Apparently, Mithun and four of his friends had gone for a swim.

Mithun had been swept away and one of his friends had dived in to try to save him. The friend had been saved but Mithun had drowned.

My friends and I immediately started off for the dock on a Hercules cycle. When we reached there, it was desolate. Panting desperately, I gazed at the majestic Periyar. The river flowed serenely, as if nothing was wrong. My friend was hiding somewhere in her depths. Tears welled up in my eyes. The sun was playing hide and seek with the coconut leaves on the opposite shore. *God! Has Mithun vanished forever from my life?*

Somehow, I struggled through the night. I reached the dock again early in the morning. By that time, a massive crowd was thronging the riverbank. Despite many searches, Mithun had not been found. After long hours, I returned to the school numbly. The day dragged on endlessly.

I went back to the dock again the next day. The fire force and police were present on the shore. It was the third day since Mithun had gone missing. I had accepted that he would never come back. When the river of sorrow overflowed in my heart, Mithun wouldn't be around to console me with a gentle pat on my back, whispering, 'Just let it go.'

The words of the famous S. Janaki's song cleaved my heart: 'Ninte ormakalil veenudanju pidayunnu njan [I lie broken, shuddering in your memories…]'

A man who was searching the river shouted suddenly, 'Here! Found him!'

Despite the din of the crowd, I clearly heard those words. I managed to wriggle my way through the horde. Though the cops and fire force were around, it was a select group of men who had discovered the corpse. Apparently, they specialized in such tasks. Nobody moved despite one of the men's shout that Mithun's body had been sighted. Everyone was busy covering their noses. Somehow, I did not feel the stench. I was staring at the man. Mithun was near him, unable to see any of us.

'Someone, come quick! Help me!'

When I looked around, everybody was muffling their noses and faces with towels. Not a person responded. The man who found Mithun was enraged. 'You useless fuckers! Not anyone to help?'

I understood that he and his friends were stone drunk. Why fear anyone when there was water – or liquor, rather – inside one's body and outside? The men in the water were hollering.

'Fuck! Someone ... step into the water!' The men mocked the crowd, knowing no one would come.

'Shall I come, Chetta?' The words sprang out of my mouth unknowingly.

'Anyone will do. Come on.'

I dove into the river. There was no thought in my mind except that I had to find Mithun as soon as I could. I was wearing my school uniform. Soon, I reached the man's side. It was then that I saw the half-submerged corpse. The man asked me to grasp the legs. Silently, I obeyed.

When I had fought with Mithun, I had clutched at his collar. Later, I had walked with my arm around his shoulder. I had known the warmth of his friendship. Now, my hands were holding his frozen limbs. I was touching a dead body for the first time, and feeling such overwhelming love.. I felt my hold slipping. Were my hands trembling due to emotion? No, the skin was coming off! The fetid stench of rotting flesh filled the air. Those on the riverbank had their faces covered. Many looked nauseous. Only the men in the river and I were impassive.

I looked at Mithun's face. It was not the face I knew. I could hardly recognize the frozen face of my best friend. The body was badly decomposed. Though my hands quivered and my mind was tottering on the edges of panic, an ineffable strength flowed into me from somewhere. Nothing deterred me – neither the overpowering odour of the corpse nor my memories of Mithun. I followed the instructions of the men and laid the corpse on the shore. I stood staring at the water for a while afterwards.

My eyes scanned the retrievers of the corpse: the *asanmar* or masters were what I thought of them as and also what I called them. After the turmoil and shock of having recovered Mithun's body left me, my attention was caught by the strange men. There were five or six of them. They were fearlessly drinking and smoking in front of the police. How come they were so intrepid?

I was a scaredy-cat. Absolutely terrified of cops and ghosts. I was awed at the sight of the corpse collectors. They were drunk out of their minds. Nobody was even wearing gloves! I was dumbstruck.

'We are leaving, brat!'

When they bid farewell, I ran after them.

'Let me come with you.' An innate urge to be part of this group – which seemed utterly fearless of cops and ghosts and people – pulled me towards them.

'No way! Stay back.'

The men vanished from the scene. I was clueless about their destination.

❧

My body reeked of a foul smell. It was the final gift of my dearest friend, destined to drown forever in my memories. His bodily remains stuck to my clothes. It was as if Mithun was embracing me even after death.

Covering their noses, my friends warned me, 'You are stinking terribly!'

The corpse was wrapped in a mat woven from palm leaves. I followed the ambulance to the Aluva Government Hospital. On reaching the place, the cops needed help to shift the body to the mortuary. Nobody came forward. Again, I volunteered. The cops held Mithun's head and I held his legs.

After we deposited the corpse carefully, the police men patted me on the back. 'What's your name?'

'Vinu.'

'Keep this with you.'

They gave me some cash. I refused to touch the money. My eyes were overflowing.

'Your clothes are filthy. Go and change. Where are you studying, boy?'

'St Mary's.'

'In which class?'

'Tenth.'

The police men treated me very affectionately.

I did not go to school that day. Neither did I return to my father's ironing shop. I went home. Taking off my soiled uniform, I soaked it in soapy water. I had seen my father washing clothes. I removed my best friend as best as I could from the shirt that clung close to my body. But he was still thrashing around inside my heart.

'Why is your dress on the clothesline?' My mother snapped at me in the evening.

'Amma, I slipped when I went to the market.'

I got a few slaps, but it ended there, thankfully.

At night, when I lay down to sleep, Mithun reappeared in my thoughts. A medley of memories: how we met for the first time, how we got into a scuffle, how we became best friends, how we collected matchbox pictures, how we watched movies in Zeenat Theatre … Every scene that had transpired from the morning flashed through my mind. I was no longer afraid of death or dead bodies. The very first corpse that I touched had buried all my terrors under the earth. That was a mystifying, strange night.

⁂

I witnessed my first accident later. I was on my way to school. As I stepped into the main road from a pathway, I noticed something odd under the thick grass on the side. It was a severed arm, still bleeding profusely. To be truthful, I was indifferent. I picked it up like a curious object and walked forward. In a short while, I saw a posse of policemen. A student at my school had been run over by a speeding vehicle. It was his arm that had been flung into the shrubs. The police were shifting the corpse when I offered them the missing arm.

My body was covered with blood. I did not care at all. The students ran away on seeing me. The policemen were not aware that the missing arm had been tossed so far away. I realized the weight of a severed arm for the first time.

I met Sub-Inspector (SI) Babu Sir of Aluva Station that day. 'Smart boy! What's your name?' He patted me on my back.

'Vinu.'

'Whenever you need anything, come to the station.'

The hefty police officer with an imposing moustache hugged me. I can never properly express the pride I felt in that moment.

Every kid was afraid of the police in those days. There was no reason for such nervousness. Perhaps, the thick, curved, intimidating moustaches of the cops had a role to play. I cuddled the police officer like a kitten. I noticed that I hardly reached his waist.

If the police officer treated me so kindly on recovering a limb, imagine the respect the asanmar, the masters, would be given? My admiration for the masters grew by leaps and bounds. I decided to join them; I was fifteen years old and studying in the tenth standard.

6

Under the Tree of Consciousness

There are certain people who transform your life after a single encounter. However, nobody can predict where or when one might meet them. Not everyone is likely to meet such people. But I can affirm something: there are certain humans in my life who are special. They are my masters. They ushered me into my life's work.

It was not easy to find the masters. Nobody knew where they stayed. As mentioned earlier, I had met them while recovering Mithun's body. Suffice it to say that I was impressed by their boldness and devil-may-care attitude. Where on earth would I search for them? I was clueless about their names or address. But the police knew their whereabouts. They told me, 'Wherever a dead body turns up, just check in the market nearby.'

I started visiting the Aluva market. Two birds with one stone: one could collect matchbox pictures and potentially catch a glimpse of the masters! How else could I find the location of those anonymous men?

Every child wants to be seen as a hero by the world. Some acquire fame by excelling in studies or arts. Some by extreme waywardness. I had no remarkable talent to boast of, but my yearning to be admired by those around remained strong. Following the path of the masters seemed to be the best route to accomplishing my aim. When everybody shivered in their pants at the mere mention of the word 'police', the masters stood with absolute nonchalance in front of the cops, did they not? They drank and smoked fearlessly when the law-keepers were around. The men spewed filthy abuses fearlessly. Nobody dared to speak to them. If I joined their cohort, I would also acquire a spine. That's how my internal monologue went.

I would play truant and skip school to search for the masters at the market. But despite many attempts, I never saw them. I wandered through the railway station, market and even visited a place called Uliyannoor, across the Periyar. I would return frustrated every day. Though I wasn't familiar with the word 'depression', that word perfectly captures my state of mind from those days.

One day, when I was returning from one of my searches, I encountered the masters under the railway overbridge near Aluva St Xavier's College. They had temporarily settled in the space under the bridge. I stood dazzled at meeting them unexpectedly.

'Get lost! Don't loiter around.' One of them warned sternly.

'It is that boy!' Someone recognized me.

'Which boy?'

'The boy who helped in pulling the body from Periyar.'

The others were indifferent on hearing that explanation. 'So what? He cannot come here.'

The masters drove me away. I unwillingly left the place. However, I was thrilled to have discovered their location. I went back after two days.

'What do you want?' they asked.

I was silent.

'This is no place for children. Go to school. If you stay, someone will kidnap you.'

'As if I am a small child whom anyone can kidnap!' I retorted.

'Smart aleck! What's your business here? Do you see our clothes? If you stay, you will start stinking. Go away.'

'I want to stay with you,' I pleaded.

But they were adamant.

On the third day, I went again. There was nobody around. I stayed put. The masters arrived after some time. That day, they became friendlier. The men asked my name, details of the school I went to and what class I was in.

'No beedi left!' One of them said suddenly.

'I will get it for you,' I jumped in eagerly.

'Okay, send him.'

They gave me ₹5. I was ecstatic. Three rolls of Roja beedi. ₹1.5 for one roll. I returned with 50 paisa and three rolls of beedi.

'You can keep the balance,' one of them said.

In those days, 25 paisa was the usual bus fare. My father used to give me 50 paisa daily. Instead of catching the bus, I would spend the money on sweets. After walking to school, I would skip classes. Some would watch movies at Zeenat Theatre. Some would stand gaping in front of the girls' school. I would run off to where the masters stayed. If anyone questioned me, I would fib that I was going to collect matchbox pictures at the market. Soon, the masters became an inseparable part of my life. They started liking me.

During lunch time, they would ask: 'Don't you want food?'

'Yes.'

'Come, join us.'

Everyone ate together from a single plantain leaf. I remembered dumping boiled green grams into the bucket of rice gruel and gobbling it down with my seniors. But this was different. There was no cleanliness around. The men would not even bother to wash their hands. It was a revealing experience as far as I was concerned. I would also grab a fistful of food. I used to be finicky by nature, but my fastidiousness left me after meeting the masters.

Once the ice melted, they started sharing stories with me. I would ask questions: 'Don't you feel afraid to lift the corpses?'

They would grin.

When they were drunk, their tales would pour forth – about gathering shattered bodies from rail tracks, bringing down the dead bodies that were hanging, how the police gave them food and money ... They would speak about the good hearts and kindness of the cops. Never did they speak ill about anybody or criticize each other.

The truth is that I had only ever seen people accusingly pointing fingers at each other – at home, at school and in the village. How rare to find people who never found fault with anyone! Everybody loves to bitch about other people. Though cruelly treated as outcasts by society, the masters never sunk to that level. It was something which astounded me.

When they were in a good mood, I would enquire: 'Are ghosts for real?'

'Of course! There is one standing just behind you.'

'Don't taunt me, please.' I would get slightly scared.

'The ghosts are real! Might catch you.'

They would make a joke of everything.

After talking to them, I realized one thing. One should have faith not in ghosts, but in those who offer us food. My school taught us that it was God who gave us our daily bread. But it was the police who gave sustenance to the masters. Even liquor was akin to food as far as they were concerned. That is how I concluded that the cops were gods. Later, it turned out to be the holy truth in my case.

Those were the days of arrack and toddy. The masters could not survive without liquor. They did not bother about the type of drink so long as it was intoxicating enough. Sometimes, they would send me to buy drinks. There was a shop near the Aluva railway station. Few talented drunkards had sketched edifying pictures on the walls. The place was notorious for attracting the town's pickpockets, rowdies and beggars. I ventured confidently into that scary area, forgetting that I was a young boy. Going there in my school uniform did not embarrass me at all. The students of St Mary's were stalwarts in all respects! The masters would pay me a rupee for my work.

Adolescence is the time when teenagers yearn to move away from their parents' influence and chart their own paths. I started feeling like I had grown up and started forging my own path. I would beseech the masters: 'Please take me along when you go to collect bodies.'

Finally, the D-day arrived.

We were seated under the railway bridge as usual. Then, the masters were called to work. One of the masters came to where we were sitting and said, 'Someone has fallen from the Thuruthu bridge into the river. We should retrieve the corpse.'

While traveling north from Aluva, the Thuruthu bridge is the first across the Periyar.

'Come with us. Your first job.' The masters smiled. We went to the spot together.

When we reached the spot we realized that the man had in fact been run over by a train. He was lying shattered on the ground. His body was splattered on the tracks and the pillar nearby. One of his legs was floating in the river flowing below.

'Can you get the leg?' the masters said, pointing at the limb.

'Yes.'

I was used to swimming in ponds, not rivers. I had stepped into the Periyar for the first time when Mithun had died; the river had been waist deep then. Now, when I reached the riverbank, I assessed that the flowing water was neck deep. The task was not too risky. The masters were standing on the bridge. In case I was in any danger, they would save me for sure.

'Go on, jump in.' The masters encouraged me.

I dove into the river. Something brushed against my hand in the first attempt. It was the man's leg, heavier than me. Somehow, I managed to swim to the shore with it. When I dragged the heavy limb out of the water, I felt giddy. Darkness rushed into my eyes. I sat down heavily on the ground. The world slowly steadied itself. The police took away the leg from my grasp, ignoring my state. As the cops arranged the shattered pieces together, the masters were standing at a distance, planning to get a drink. The cops asked one of them to accompany them in the blue Mahindra Jeep. I thought he was being arrested, but no, it was to record his statement as part of the inquest.

I understood what an inquest was in due time; it is a formal police enquiry into causes of death. It involves taking evidence from people and is referred to as *panchnama* in North India. Post-mortem is a medical formality involving cutting the body. It is mandatory for every abnormal death, including accidents. Sometimes, the authorities preserve certain organs or viscera, if there is doubt of murder or foul play. The corpse is then stitched back. The family usually receives the body after the inquest and post-mortem formalities. 'Recover the corpse. Hold it, turn it, lay it straight, wrap it up. Help the police in all these actions.' The masters taught me about the different aspects of their occupation.

Usually, the masters did not go to the hospital for the post-mortem formalities. Often, they would be given ₹500, some food and a bottle of liquor. It was enough to make all of them very happy.

They were paid ₹500 that day too. 'This belongs to you. Go ahead, take it.' They tucked the money inside my pocket. I had never seen a ₹500 note in my life. Though grubby, it was a precious ₹500 note that was lying inside my pocket! I was dumbstruck. I did not know what to say or do next. My eyes overflowed. My heart started beating faster.

After my initial shock, I regained my composure. I knew the men needed food. I ran to a nearby shop and purchased three packets of rice and curry. When I gave the balance money to the masters, they spoke affectionately: 'Keep it with you, boy! You earned it.'

Happily, I went to a famous gift shop in town and purchased my dream toy: a battery-operated car, which moved without the hassle of winding it up with a key. Also, a few notebooks. Not that I had decided to become a good student from that day onwards. If you bought notebooks for the studious ones, they would prepare notes for you for free. I still had ₹100 left after my shopping. I went home and gave it to my mother. I lied that I had picked it up from the road. My father would have probed further, so I evaded him. It was the first time in my life that I had earned wages. I really felt proud of myself then. After all, I had made some hard-earned money, while studying in tenth standard, hadn't I?

I was not closely acquainted with the police at that time. I knew only the stories the masters narrated about them. In those chronicles, the cops were good people. I fondly remembered SI Babu Sir's warm compliments when I had retrieved the severed arm of the accident victim. Every time I reminisced about that moment, it was as if a soothing, cool rain was falling on me. My hair stood on end with thrill and pride. A smile would bloom unwittingly on my face. I was determined to help the police whenever I could.

The masters shifted camp very often. They had no permanent place to stay. They camped under different overbridges. They never disclosed their next location to me or to anyone else. As far as they were concerned, they had no ties in the world. I was supposed to find them whenever they moved away. In those days, we did not have mobile phones. In fact, I ended up losing touch with them for some time.

After some time, I met the masters again on the day of the infamous murder case in Aluva. It was later known as the 'Cecily Case', where two people were poisoned by a woman named Cecily. The masters collected the corpses. The crowd was immense. I felt at peace on seeing them and refused to leave their side. When I did not return home after five, my father informed my elder brother. He came to find me. I was beaten black and blue when I reached home. My family members had been mad with worry. My brother had fanned the flames with his backbiting.

The next time I participated in collecting a corpse was during a train accident. The train had run over the victim and nobody had any clue about it. It was due to the intolerable stench that people finally noticed. That was the day I became aware of the foul smell that emanates from a dead body. In Mithun's case, my focus was somewhere else.

When I reached the accident spot with the masters, the corpse was putrid and crawling with maggots. 'What should I do?' I queried.

'Will you vomit?'

'No.'

'Just spread a sheet.'

It was a woman's body. I concentrated on how the masters worked, ignoring the fetid smell. That day, I followed the cops to the mortuary in the government hospital; I helped shift the cadaver. I had presumed that the work ended after removing the corpse from the site. I had no inkling about the post-mortem formality. That day, I became cognizant of the next steps.

The policeman began giving me instructions. 'Untie the sheet.'

I obeyed. Flies and maggots were feasting on the lifeless body.

'Move the body to the table.' The policeman went out after instructing me.

Singlehandedly, I managed to lift the dead woman's body on to the post-mortem table. When the cop returned with two men, I informed him: 'The body is on the table, Sir.'

'You did it by yourself?' he asked, shocked.

The other policeman noticed my school uniform. 'You are a school boy. Who asked you to enter the room?' He was trying to scare me off.

'Sir, this boy is part of Velayudhan's group. He is a big help. Let him stay.' Once the first cop explained, the situation changed. My joy knew no bounds on being referred as a 'help'!

Afterwards, in every case, I went to the hospital. I would loiter around until the post-mortem was done. In those days, they kept the carcass on ice. I started helping during the inquest procedure – tilting and turning the body as needed. After a few cases, I became quite an expert. Even without any instructions, I started following the standard steps. I knew exactly what would be recorded when the inquest process was carried out. The policemen became very comfortable with me.

After the procedures in the hospital, they would tell me: 'Come around to the station, lad.' Beaming proudly, I would proceed to the police station.

Then they would give me ₹200 and say, 'Keep the cash.' One day when the masters arrived upon hearing of an incident, I was already at the police station. 'The bloody fucker is here,' they acknowledged me, affectionately. It was their practice to use obscene words to address anyone.

Then, one of the masters said, 'Sir, you don't need our services nowadays, do you?'

The police officers laughed: 'He is your disciple, isn't he? We can understand that from his work.'

The masters seemed very pleased with the answer. I felt happy and proud. The police officers gave me ₹200 per case in those days. When all eight of the masters together received ₹500, a mere lad like me was given 200! More than the money, it was their encouraging words that delighted me: 'Drop in at the station whenever you can.' In those days, I would wear two shirts to school. When I went to recover a body, I would remove my white shirt.

I failed the state-level tenth standard examinations; never did I learn anything at school. I went to check the results by myself. When I went home, I lied that I had passed. My father said that since my marks would not be sufficient to enrol in a college, I should start working. He sent me to Mithun's father's service centre. As mentioned before, it was located in front of Zeenat Theatre. When the work at the service centre was over, I would go to the nearest police station. To get away from the service centre, I would pray that some corpses turned up somewhere. Usually, there were three or four cases of untimely death every week.

One day, a police jeep screeched to a halt at the service centre. Someone had died, having fallen into the gutter at Aluva market. The vehicle had been sent to fetch me. When I reached the spot, I stated confidently, 'I will handle it myself.'

In the gutter, where faecal waste flowed, I stood waist deep in the filth and tried to lift up the cadaver. It did not budge. Somehow, I managed to grab a leg and dragged the body out of the sewer.

The masters came to know about the incident and said, 'We are proud of you, boy. You did a good job.'

I would visit them whenever I could. Either alone or with the masters, I would help the police collect dead bodies. One day, Mithun's father came to know about my profession.

'Someone who gathers corpses has no place here!' he shouted.

He was ruthless. I was gravely upset. My eyes overflowed with tears. Mithun's father had no idea that it was I who had retrieved his son's corpse. I turned to leave. Suddenly, he was filled with pity. 'Where are you off to?'

I did not reply. Just wiped my eyes.

'How can you just leave like that? Your father entrusted you in my care.'

I did not wait any longer. 'I am leaving.'

I went straight to the police station.

'What happened to you? Why is your face so sad?' the SI enquired anxiously.

'I was not at the service centre when they were washing the car. They got annoyed at me. Asked me not to come anymore.' I lied blatantly.

'Let me talk to him. Come along.'

'No, Sir. I don't want to work there anymore.'

The officer talked to me for a long time. It was then that he realized that my father was Purushottaman who pressed clothes for a living. Most of the cops at Aluva were familiar with him. They got their uniforms ironed at his shop.

Achan's heart broke when he learned I had left the car wash centre. Then, he took me to a paint shop at Ernakulam for work. I would travel daily in a private bus. One day, a bus coming from the other side crushed a man on the road. The incident happened near the Kalamassery Police Station. When the cops arrived, I intervened: 'I will handle it, sir.'

Gathering the shattered bits of the corpse, I wrapped the remains in a mat made of screw-pine leaves. We transported the dead body to the hospital. Three policemen gave me money that day.

I had not noticed him but the owner of the paint shop had witnessed me gathering the splintered cadaver. The next day, when I reached my workplace, the man raised a question: 'Where were you yesterday?'

'Had fever.'

'Don't come to work anymore.'

It was the second time that I was fired from my job for gathering corpses. I was familiar with all the bus stops and bus routes of the area. I managed to get a job in a bus. The driver's name was Muthu. I was supposed to stay near the bus's door and ring the bell when it had to stop. Seeing my confidence, the owner handed over the conductor's bag to me. That evening, he counted the currency wads and found it to be exactly what it should have been. I was promoted from helper to conductor. Actually, I did well in the job.

One day, the cops saw me at the bus station. 'Vinu, we hardly get to see you nowadays. Do visit the station sometimes.'

I left the conductor's job on hearing those words. The policemen bought a mobile phone for me. 'Keep the phone. Will call when we require help.'

It was an Escotel connection. Nobody in the village had a phone then. The year was 2002. In the thirty-five houses of our colony, I was the only one who owned a mobile. I would hide it at home and use the phone only when I stepped out.

One day, I was at the Ashokapuram ground and my mobile phone rang. Everybody's attention turned to me. The phone was big and the trilling was loud. I preened around happily.

'Hello, who is it?' I asked, rather pompously.

'This is the Aluva Sub-Inspector. Vinu, a jeep will come to pick you up. There is some urgent work.'

The jeep came in a short time. I got inside. Some people then ran to my house frantically. 'The police have arrested Vinu. They took him away in a jeep.' Amma started weeping and ran to the station.

When the cops and I reached the station after disposing of the corpse, my mother was there and wailed on seeing me. The cops consoled my crying mother. 'We did not arrest Vinu. There were some festoons strung high in the school. We got him to remove those.'

I was immediately packed off home with Amma. The news of my so-called arrest had spread throughout the colony. I hadn't done anything wrong, but I was portrayed as a criminal. My mother refused to let me leave the house after that incident. Time went by. My eighteenth birthday was nearing. The year was 2003.

'Ever since you started working in the buses, these cases have been tailing you. No more jobs in buses!' My father declared firmly. I had never told my family that I had stopped working as a conductor. I was secretly busy helping the cops with corpses all day.

I then started working as a cleaner in a lorry. The driver had heard some rumours about me. He started asking me questions about death. The man would attempt to inveigle information out of me that I didn't usually share with anyone. One day, I confessed about my profession to him, and he duly gossiped about it to an autorickshaw driver, who was my father's acquaintance.

'Let us buy an auto for Vinu,' the man, who kept my secret safe, suggested to my father. He agreed.

But one needed a licence to drive an auto, so I went to the police station. 'Sir, I need a licence.'

'Why not? Go and meet the motor vehicle inspector. Tell him that I sent you.' The SI was kind.

The motor vehicle inspector asked me to join a driving school and clear the mandatory tests. I was not yet eighteen. When I turned eighteen in 2003, I cleared all the four driving tests. Because of the police's involvement, getting a licence became easy.

My father bought a '99 model Bajaj petrol autorickshaw for me. My neighbour (the same autorickshaw driver who was my father's acquaintance) and I would go for rounds. Usually, the cops caught people who violated rules. But they never troubled me for anything. They would simply ignore me. I usually parked my autorickshaw at the police station. I would also accompany the police for handling dead bodies, often travelling in the jeep. In fact, I would be with them till six in the evening. I was driving my auto and doing police work on the side. The handling of corpses took more of my time than the auto-driving work.

In the past, the masters used to call me for work. Now, I started calling them to join me. Whenever the task was beyond a single person, I would invite them to come along. I would also drop them to where they were staying in my autorickshaw. We would share the wages among ourselves. I was proud to be a disciple who got his masters decent money and work. They were also pleased with me.

7

The Hunted

Slowly, I was getting ostracized by society. I did not understand what my crime was or why everyone loathed me. It was later that the realization dawned on me: society is a cat that pretends to be tame but cruelly plays with its victim, like a cat with a mouse. It shall not kill at a single go, but relishes the torture, cut by cut.

Though I tried to park my vehicle at an autorickshaw stand, all of them shooed me away. They even drove me from Ashokapuram stand, in my own village. Most people knew about my profession. They gave me the nickname Shavamvari, Corpse Collector.

After being called Peppatti (or Rabid Dog), the second moniker was Corpse Collector. The two epithets, given at two different phases of my life, were striking. The first did not perturb me much, even during my school days. But the second, being called Shavamvari, played havoc with my life.

On seeing me, people would grumble: 'Oh, don't you know him? Collects corpses for a living.' I would be at the forefront whenever an untimely death struck the city. Since the locals started seeing me in unnerving situations, the bitterness of the gossip increased. In the past, nobody bothered much about me, since I had the protective cover of the masters. I used to do my work hiding behind them. But while working independently, I became conspicuous. Initially, I would use caps and masks to evade notice. But people easily recognized me. Even the relatives of those who died needed me only for collecting the corpses. I became a pariah after that. An abhorred man.

Shopkeepers looked at me contemptuously. They would be very considerate with other customers: 'What do you need, please?' But when it came to me, it was always a disrespectful order: 'You wait here.' Mostly, they chased me away. I was denied tea at the tea-shop.

After such experiences I understood why the masters would pitch their camps under railway bridges. Time had been relentlessly cruel to them, and now Time was treating me, their shadow, similarly. Nothing had changed. Whatever treatment had been doled out to the masters was now being meted out to me, with the same intensity and measure.

I am also a human being; someone who has feelings. The loathing I faced, even from those dear and near, hurt me intensely. I would yearn for someone to appreciate my work; someone apart from the police. I remembered Namboodiri Sir of my school then.

When I was in the tenth standard, I had gone to help with a corpse near my house. It was a body which was a few days old. The masters and I had toiled to collect the cadaver. Nobody noticed me since a band of cops were surrounding us. But one man gazed at me with wonder from the crowd. It was my school teacher – Namboodiri Sir.

He called me near him, the next day. 'Vinu, what you do is undoubtedly good. Truly worth all blessings. But nobody should know about it at school. Your studies shall end immediately. Do not wear your uniform while doing this work.'

Namboodiri Sir guided me sincerely that day. He said nice things about me and my occupation. Yet, I felt wounded. He had said: 'Nobody should know about it ...'What did that imply? Though I did not comprehend what my teacher had said then, much later, after seeing society's attitude, I recognized the truth of those prescient words. Society looked at my profession as something forbidden and depraved. Nobody, except the police and the masters, ever appreciated my work. Even the neighbour who once rode with me in my autorickshaw addressed me as Shavamvari. The man lived in perfect resonance with the society that treated me as an outcast.

I was discriminated against by everybody. No hotel allowed me entry. Since I was friendly with the masters, the locals treated me as a vagrant too. Drunkard, immoral, dirty: the encomiums were many. Above all, a 'corpse collector'. Everyone loathed my sight. The hatred and vehemence were staggering. My parents never spoke a word. They refused to believe what they had heard, denying the truth until they saw it for themselves. 'Been hearing many complaints about you recently,' Acchan would remark occasionally.

However, his trust in me was very deep. Acchan would boast to his relatives and friends, 'I shall educate my son. He will achieve what I could not.' He got to know about my failure in the tenth exams very late. Back then I had gone to check the results by myself, as I mentioned earlier. Eventually, the locals started mocking my parents because of my work. When they walked along the road, the taunts would begin: 'There goes the Corpse Collector's mother!' or 'There goes the Corpse Collector's father!'

As Acchan would freeze, mortified to the core, the villagers would surround him. 'Your son gathers corpses, doesn't he? How else shall we address you?' Acchan would be traumatized at their derision. It was natural for a father to suffer when society pointed fingers at his son.

One day, a man collapsed and died inside the village tea-shop. I wrapped his corpse in a mattress. Acchan was observing me from a distance. When I reached home, he asked me: 'Why do you do such things?'

'It is a good thing that I did. I helped the man, didn't I?'

Acchan could not accept what I said. 'Don't do this work anymore!'

He bought me yet another autorickshaw. As I was busy with helping the police, I could never concentrate on my job as an auto driver. Each time there were inevitably huge losses and eventually I would have to sell my autos. However, Acchan had a strong conviction that *this time* I would forsake my 'forbidden' job and return to the relatively decent profession of an auto driver. So, he kept on buying me autos one by one, taking loans from banks. Unfortunately, I could never repay the loans and always ended up losing the autos.

There have been five autorickshaws in my life. Each time I got a new auto I had to move away from where I plied my vehicle, due to ostracization. Nobody would let me join their auto stand. Whenever I approached the nearby stand in the village where I lived they spoke fervently: 'No way! You are friends with dirty rascals. Vinu, you handle corpses. We are not interested in getting infected with some dreadful disease. Nobody wants to die. Get lost!'

Nobody wanted me around.

I started travelling to Ernakulam, hoping that nobody would recognize me in the city. But many people did. I was the man who collected dead bodies that were found hanging in lodges.

By the year 2017, I was working independently collecting corpses for the Police. I used to request my masters's help for certain cases. A new bridge had come over Aluva market by that time. The masters finally got a good resting place. They would spread the sheet and base board underneath and sleep in peace.

When the autorickshaw experiment did not take off, the cops intervened. 'Vinu, you should drive an ambulance. Your negative reputation will disappear overnight. Nobody will care what you do once you drive an ambulance. Everything becomes part of the job.'

In 2018, the police officers made me join an ambulance service named 'Biomic'. My work was focused around Ernakulam. One day, an auto driver died by suicide, jumping from the Venduruthy bridge. The corpse ended up floating near the shipyard. I lifted the dead body out of the water. That was my last case at Ernakulam. The police officers asked me to return to Aluva. I joined 'Amma Ambulance Service' run by Linoy Chettan there. I got a new nickname 'Amma Ambulance Vinu'.

The 'Shavamvari' epithet persisted even then. There was no shortage of scorn or cold-shouldering, even when I drove an ambulance. Everyone seemed to know about my occupation. All hotels and shops forbade entry to me. Once, I entered a famous hotel in the city. An employee, hailing from my village, recognized me. He came running to my side. 'This is no place for corpse gatherers. Scram!' I left the hotel without a word.

On another occasion, a bakery was being inaugurated at Aluva pump junction. Everyone in the audience was being offered a piece of cake and a cup of tea. I hoped that nobody would identify me in that massive crowd. Even amid that throng, someone looked at me and started shouting at the top of his voice: 'This goddamn rascal has come after lifting corpses! If this sort is allowed in this place, how will we stay here?'

The security man came running, slapped me viciously on the head and said, 'Get lost now!'

He drove me away like a dog.

I went to the masters, overwhelmed by my humiliation and desolation. 'Don't be sad, Vinu. How far will these fellows go? You see it daily, don't you? There will be nobody to cast a backward glance at them after a certain time, except us. Just let it go.'

They infused me with some positive energy. But I was far from consoled. Though I tried hard, the vessel of my sorrow was brimming over.

I went to the police station. An officer comforted me. 'Vinu, sometimes even we are treated like slaves. Endure such abuses. Please have some food with me.'

Sir served me food. While we chatted, a call came. Someone had hanged himself. The officer asked me to go with the police team. Embittered, I replied negatively: 'I am not coming, Sir.'

'You can't give up so easily. Come on, Vinu.'

The police knew that working made me happy. When we neared the location, I realized it was Ashokapuram, my village.

'Sir, my house is located near the ground. Everybody knows me here,' I panicked.

'You ignore everything. I shall handle the situation.'

The Officer took me to the house. The woman who had hanged herself was the wife of my father's friend. People were glaring at me as if I was a monster. I went to the hospital after bringing the body down. When I reached home after the post-mortem, all hell broke loose.

'You better stop this job,' Acchan yelled. He was unyielding.

I stood silently.

'I shall get you employment in some workshop.'

'I will not get peace unless I do this work,' I said frankly.

A spate of hits, slaps and chaos ensued.

Over time, I was treated as an outsider even in my home. Even Acchan stopped expressing any affection towards me. The locals had made my parents' lives hell because of me. They could not tolerate that dishonour. What sin had they committed to endure such mockery?

The locals would not even sell me a soda. 'You stink! No soda for you.'

Even when someone else was gulping down water, the shopkeepers would decline my request. 'There is no glass for you here.'

Sometimes they would just shut their eyes and shoo me away, gesticulating disgustedly with their hands. I was boycotted by all the shops around my village. If I coughed, everybody would become frantically worried. Those were the days when people were afraid of catching HIV. The less said about the situation, the better. When I went to Aluva town, the situation did not change.

❧

'Friends' sounded like a word from my previous birth. Just memories. After I started gathering corpses, even my old friends started avoiding me. They would make it a point to step away from the road if I chanced to walk that way. Only Anas would say, 'How are you?' If he talked more, he would also face social boycott.

If I went to the temple, everyone would chase me away viciously. 'Why are you loitering around? This is no place for someone impure.' Not just humans, even God started rejecting me. I could not even attend the temple festival. Not a single home was open to me. From the tenth standard, I had stopped visiting the houses of relatives. When I walked on the road, someone would holler, 'There goes the Shavamvari!' Spiteful hands would cuff me on my head.

If I sat somewhere, people would assemble to beat me up. At Ashokapuram ground, the playing children would surround me and unleash an assault. 'Run away, scoundrel. This place is meant for us.' On seeing me anywhere, people would chase me away like a mad dog, showering filthy abuses and slaps. I became a pariah in Aluva. A socially ostracized man.

One day the police team went to a shop. I was with them.

One of the policemen said, 'Four sherbets.'

The shopkeeper gave three sherbets for the three policemen. Nothing for me.

'Where is his sherbet?'

'Sir, er…'

'You better give him a glass!'

When the officers shouted, I was offered some sherbet. In an old, grubby glass! The way the shopkeeper took the glass back from my hand and those from the cops spoke volumes. I was treated like a patient infected by smallpox, leprosy, syphilis or AIDS.

The crowd took care to touch only my head even while attacking me! They would harm me at every occasion, even a festive one. Without any reason, the rabble would start bashing me up. I never had the capacity to fight back, in the past or now.

In those days when relatives came to invite us to weddings, they would ask my parents: 'Purusha, Ambi, you shall reach on time, won't you?' Turning to me, they would comment, 'Vinu, you shall not be coming, right?'

It was never 'Will you come, Vinu?'

I would get crushed at that venom.

Once, very joyfully, full of eagerness, I attended a wedding. The girl was a close relative, like an elder sister to me. There are rituals which require the bride's brother to wash the feet of the groom and garland him. Though I was present, I was not allowed to do those auspicious rites. Instead, a distant relative was made to do those. I remained silent. Somehow, I had hoped that this household would behave differently with me. My hope lay shattered. When I was not treated as a brother, a relative or even an acquaintance, I decided to have the food and leave the place without delay.

After washing my hands, I sat in the row of guests for the traditional wedding feast. The plantain leaf was laid before me. Rice and curries were served. I was about to eat the first fistful of food when a relative of the girl noticed me; he knew me and my profession very well. He walked slowly towards me. Bending close, he whispered into my ear: 'The most important event of your sister's life is happening now. We don't want you to be part of it. Leave immediately.'

My face downcast, I got up. I don't know how many were watching. My eyes were overflowing, so I didn't see anyone. I knew that nobody would take up my case. I left the venue, which was filled with relatives and villagers. It was as if I had committed some grave crime. From that day onwards, I have never participated in any public event, neither marriages nor any other functions.

Except the police officers, everybody abhorred my presence. The staff at the casualty unit at hospitals would shoot daggers at me. On seeing me carry the corpse, they would frown and gripe: 'From where does the rogue dig them up?' The bystanders at the hospital, who came to take care of patients, started driving me away.

My family was not there to hold me close. No friends to speak with. There wasn't anyone with whom I could share my heavy burden. When the agony became overwhelming, I would sit alone and cry. Smoking beedis was a relief. I would drive aimlessly in my autorickshaw. After parking the vehicle somewhere desolate, I would sit and smoke silently.

The masters and the police would find time to listen to me occasionally. If someone misbehaved with me at the auto stand, the cops would seize his vehicle. Some officers let me pour out my heart before them. But their jobs were transferable and many could not stay friends with me for long.

My heart became a tinderbox, ready to explode at any moment – a volcano needs an outlet for what is churning within. My life was not valued by those living around me. Only the dead needed me. That was the lone thought which prevented me from killing myself.

Burned by the fiery gale of rejection and shuddering in the relentless torrent of hatred, I was lost, wandering through lands where I never belonged. I could feel my sanity threatening to leave me, like birds in flight. I was utterly helpless. Every human being on this earth who lacks a foothold of soil to call his own, or a friendly shoulder to lay his head on, is a destitute like I was.

A few police officers became angels of mercy as I battled this inexpressible pain. Their homes were open to me night and day. I revealed my sorrows to them. Nobody had any ready-made solution. Instead, they shared their own pains with me. I felt a touch of soothing coolness while listening to them. Unlike them, nobody crushed me underfoot, threatened my family, ordered my transfer or made me do house work. I understood that every profession had its woes. Every human had their problems.

Revisiting the paths that I had treaded so far, a stark truth struck me. People recognized me and ostracized me during daytime. So light was the ultimate issue. I was free at night. Darkness became my consolation. I started detesting the hours of day after that insight. The day belongs to those who cast me off. The day detested me. If only I had a boon to vanish during the day ... I could wander around without anyone seeing me; appearing only when work called. Or better, I could carry corpses while staying invisible.

At night, I was blissful. Nobody could see me. Darkness belonged to me. Darkness guarded me. Darkness embraced me. Darkness was not for sleeping – it was for celebrating my freedom.

I stopped sleeping at night. I would drop off to sleep when the rooster crowed at dawn. I would wake up when the sun became intensely hot. This practice continues till today.

AMBULANCE

8

A Marriage by Deceit

My family started searching for a bride for me when I turned twenty-one in 2006. My reputation was getting increasingly spoilt every day. They were apprehensive that with each passing day, the chances of getting me married would be slimmer.

But not a single proposal went right. Every time the girl's family started their enquiries about me, the villagers would maliciously intercede. The chronic gossipers relished damaging human lives, especially mine. Not a single person spoke well about me: 'Vinu? Couldn't you find anybody else for your daughter? He is a corpse collector!'

The locals enthusiastically spread their venom and ensured that no wedding proposal fructified. Even our relatives avoided my house. It was me, and my profession, which were behind our isolation.

What could be done? Mine was an accursed life. For my relatives, my life was a travesty and made them laugh. My parents were devastated by that scorn.

Some of my Valiyachan's (father's elder brother) children were in government service or were abroad, in professions like engineering and nursing. They were a part of the upper strata of society. It is common practice that the rich disparage the poor. Well, it happened in our family too.

My family was depressed because my marriage wasn't happening. Seeing their pain, I too became affected. But I could do nothing. In a few years, after a spate of rejections, I gave up hope.

Finally, the police came forward to help me. Usually, the girl's family members come to verify the boy's antecedents in his locality. In my case, it was Ashokapuram and its vicinity. The cops started patrolling the area. The sight of the police jeep and the cops' rounds became a daily affair. Our area was infested with petty criminals. On seeing the police jeep, nobody wouldn't dare to step outside their houses. Nobody knew who the law enforcers were after! Those who had something to hide became wary. In reality, the police had ensured their *bandobast* just to help me.

My mother had gone to Vypin to sell fish. There, she met a girl whom she liked at first sight. When she proposed marriage, the girl's family was ready. They came to our home, as was expected. The visit was successful. Owing to the police rounds, nothing untoward happened.

My marriage was solemnized. I never disclosed my real work to the girl. In her eyes, I was an autorickshaw driver. The ambulance-driving part of my life, which I have mentioned earlier, was in the future at this time.

After the wedding, wherever the local women met one another – near the water tap for example – there was a lot of gossip about me. There were two public taps for the thirty-five houses in the colony. When they stood waiting for their turn, in the morning and evening, the women slandered me in front of my wife. She never took anything seriously. Even when some said things to her face, she refused to believe it until she saw the truth with her own eyes. Neither did she pester me with any questions. My wife did her best to adjust but eventually things changed. She became suspicious about me. Somehow, we lived together, despite her nagging doubts. I became the main topic of our discussions. The conversations turned into fights.

There is a proverb in my land: 'When a man marries, he gets blindfolded; when he begets a child, his legs are bound.' A married man has to turn a blind eye to many of his wife's actions. And when he becomes a father, and more responsible, all his freedom is curtailed. I was in such a condition. It was not because I had married. It was because I had hidden my true personality from my wife. Afraid of her constant suspicions, I soon stopped stepping out of the house. Only when the cops called me for work, would I move out. Four or five years passed this way. Our family life was rocky but still it endured.

On the days I handled corpses, I would take a bath in the river. I returned home only after changing my clothes. Mostly, my wife knew nothing. Her village was at Vyppinkara. I never went to her place or met her relatives. I had been there, before marriage, to gather corpses. If anyone saw me with her, the game would be up.

My mistake was that I hid my occupation. I had to lie many times to elude detection. The special, fragrant sacred mark – *kalabha kuri* – on my forehead was a sign. Whenever I worked, it would get wiped away. 'Saw Vinu at the house of the dead.' Someone would tell my wife. I would fib when my wife confronted me.

We had a little girl. But she died before she turned one. Her nostrils got blocked by an unnatural growth. She died at the hospital. We buried her in our house compound. After the baby's death, I became more solitary than before. Problems reared their heads relentlessly. One more year passed in this manner: a woman who was constantly suspicious of her husband and a man who hid the truth from his wife.

One day, the cops took me along to recover a corpse from the river. As I hauled the dead body from the waters, my wife and her friends were observing from the bridge. I did not know about their arrival. That day, my wife saw the truth with her own eyes. Whatever was burning within her, exploded in full fury. Our house was torn apart after the conflagration. Her mother came to add fuel to the fire. 'You destroyed my daughter's life! You stink of corpses!'

I shrivelled up as she heaped accusations on me. Not a word came out of my mouth. In hindsight, what happened was for the best. I was living in constant fear. I didn't have a moment's peace. Before she left, my wife gave me a last chance. I should acknowledge her generous heart. 'Either you live with me or handle corpses. Both cannot go together.'

I said to my wife what my inner voice prompted: 'It has been a few years since you came into my life. If I leave my work for your sake, I will have to search for another livelihood. I won't be able to commit myself to anything else. I shall simply become a heavy burden to myself. Compared to what we face today, more issues will crop up. My past shall follow us wherever we go. I have decided to continue with my chosen work.'

After hearing what I said, my wife walked away from my life. My wife had loved me. Scolded me. In the end, she abandoned me. It was certainly not her fault. I had lied to her. I had never disclosed the truth. I should have confessed that I was a corpse gatherer. My wife delivered an ultimatum. But I could not leave the orphaned bodies. She went away; I became alone once more.

I am happy it turned out that way. I feel only gratitude towards my wife. At the crossroads of life, one might be tempted to make impulsive choices. I now know that the path a person finally choses, proves to be the right one. Had I chosen differently, my life would have been something else. And I would never have been happy with it.

9

What the Graveyard Said

'No lie will endure forever.'

I realized the truth of the saying after my wife left me. The year was 2013 and I was twenty-eight. But a lonely human needs neither philosophy nor brutal truth – only someone to hold close.

Although life had been full of strife, after my life partner left, I lost my sleep. When everybody thrived with family, I was left all alone. First, my baby. Now, my wife. I was racked with anxiety. Sleep was the antidote to worry. But it never came my way. When I lost all hope, I got a prescription for sleeping pills from the Aluva Government Hospital.

Soon, it became a habit. First, it was a single pill. After a while, I needed two. Eventually, even after taking two pills of 10 mg each, sleep eluded me.

The doctor put his foot down. 'Vinu, if you

consume three pills, it will become an addiction. And if you take four, you will die.'

But I kept popping pills, almost vengefully. The doctor personally instructed many medical shops of Aluva: 'Listen, if Vinu asks for this medicine, do not give it to him.'

All the medical stores of the locality knew me. The doctor tapped into his contacts at the Indian Medical Association and ensured that no doctor prescribed me sleeping pills and no pharmacy gave them to me over the counter.

I started walking at night, desperate for some relief. I had no idea about my destination on those walks. When the path in front closes, many say 'I have become a burden to the earth' and kill themselves. But I did not brood about such matters. I had realized by then that my life had some other purpose. Even so, seeking some solace, I started wandering about at night. That is how I ended up at the graveyard. There, as a person who was denied even shade to rest in, I experienced the ecstasy of finding one's own space. The place was very familiar to me. As if I had known it in all my births. I recognized that the graveyard was the only place that would never malign me. With the same arms with which it embraced the dead, it hugged me close.

I went to the graveyard and confessed all my agonies, bursting into tears. For someone like me, without any sanctuary, the place became a father, mother, brother and friend. In the seclusion of the night, I slept in the graveyard. Nobody came to drive me away.

Slowly, the graveyard started answering my questions. I was told that I was not a burden to the earth and that my life had value. It was that public burial ground, near Aluva Cochin Bank, with the orphaned dead bodies, which gave me roots and planted me deeply into the earth.

I received replies to all the questions churning in my mind. The corpses were the answers. Look, in front of me were those who had travelled to many places, achieved so many things, ran about impatiently! Those who had much and those who had little were lying in the same soil, taking up just a human's sleeping space. Tomorrow, I too shall sleep in the same earth.

In that graveyard, I found the everlasting answer to the unending quest of many seekers across the ages. I understood who I was. I forgot my sorrows. The belief became strong that my life had meaning. I recognized my calling, granted to me at birth. I am the temporary handler appointed to send human beings like me back to the earth, when they turn into lifeless scraps of flesh. That is the goal of my life. Having discovered that, all the heavy burden weighing me down seemed to lift. I found the answer to my life. The mocking cry of 'Shavamvari' became delightful to my ears.

On my nightly sojourns, I witnessed much waywardness. It was in the darkness that I discovered the true colours of many dignified men who strutted about in the day. The day is a showroom that carefully displays only the best objects. In daylight, we are limited to seeing just our own selves. To see the universe, the planets and countless stars, darkness is a must. Every night, it dawned on me with clarity, that the day was just an illusion. The darkness was the truth. The graveyard gave me answers on those nights of enlightenment. After knowing the answers about life, one no longer has too many hopes and desires. Man turns into a bestial creature only due to uncontrollable desires.

My masters were behind my true awakening. It was through them that I experienced both the meaning and meaninglessness of life. My mentors had retired by then. The cops started calling me whenever they had to collect corpses. I would share my earnings with my masters. They did not have any family, sorrow or disappointment. My masters had overcome all of those. From them, I learnt that without bothering much about material gains – by simply focusing on what I was doing in the present moment – I would be more patient and effective.

Though the major part of my turmoil disappeared, getting out of the house in daylight continued to be a problem. Although I became sad when I went out during the day, suddenly a consoling thought would arise. All those who laughed at me would be around for just a few days. In the end, we shall all sleep in the same soil. Never did I think of suicide, even in my most agonizing moments. If I hanged myself, my parents would be devastated. Or I would end up mad like the character that Mohanlal depicted in *Thalavattam*! Finally, the family shall plead, 'Can you please finish him off?' What's the big deal, anyway?

Only once in my life did I yearn to die. I read about a *jawan* being mutilated badly at the border due to a grenade explosion. I have always been in awe of soldiers. The man's organs were damaged in the blast. I wished to seek euthanasia and contribute my organs – kidney, hands, all – to the man. I made an advocate email the army headquarters, stating my intention. They rejected my appeal. Apparently, there was a legal provision for transplanting organs only when a brain death occurred.

Life became easier after recognizing my designated karma: bidding farewell to abandoned dead bodies. My mind and body acquired an unfathomable lightness. It was from 2017 that I started frequenting the graveyard at night. But if you ask me when I started chatting with cadavers, I wouldn't have an exact answer. It has been quite some time now.

Conversing with corpses began at a distinct juncture of my life. Whenever I returned home after work, someone would start nitpicking. My parents reviled my occupation. When the carping and condemning began, I would retreat from the scene. In my family's eyes, I was clearly guilty. Hadn't I destroyed my father's dreams? There was nobody to talk to anywhere, at home or in the village. When I became utterly lonely – with nobody to listen to me, when my heart was on the verge of shattering in that forced isolation – unwittingly I started talking to dead bodies. It became a habit. A lone refuge in life.

I tend to be laidback by nature. But when it comes to my chosen work, I am always enthusiastic. Perhaps, corpses cause much pain to their loved ones. But they became my shelter, a haven. I can tell them anything. And I am not insistent on getting a reaction. What a human being needs on this earth is someone to listen to him. The ineffable relief one feels after opening one's heart! That's what the corpses offer me. Some call me mad because I converse with cadavers. May nobody become alone like me ...

My masters also used to chat with corpses. I followed their path. The living ones have always driven me away; they have struck my head viciously. Imagine the stinging pain of someone who suppresses all their feelings. The dead bodies would listen wordlessly to whatever I said. A man will feel close only to those who don't hurt him mentally or physically. The carcasses did not blame me or isolate me. I see the cadavers as close relatives who do not cold-shoulder me with repugnance. These carcasses cannot breathe but it does not matter to me.

Nobody stands watch over the corpses after an inquest; until the post-mortem formality is over. I would be the only one around. After the inquest, typically, the relatives and cops go their own ways. I am the person who wraps up the dead body and shifts it to the ambulance. Mostly, the dead body and I would be left to ourselves on that journey. After the post-mortem, when the body is taken to the freezer – or in the case of abandoned corpses, to the public graveyard – I am the only person around. I am fine with this. I talk to the dead body. Compared to the living, I find the dead far better. This is my testimony.

I usually encounter two categories of lifeless bodies. Either those run over by trains, shattered to bits. Or rotting, decomposing corpses, that lay unidentified somewhere. A few years ago, a mother from Trissur came to meet me. She was clutching a photograph to her heart. 'Take a look at my son's picture. Do you remember burying him, child?'

The poor mother's son had gone missing in 2008. He had been a lorry driver. Apparently, he went to take a dip in a canal at Pollachy. The man was missing ever since. He drowned when there was hardly 5 ft of water in the canal, which was 10 ft deep. The police had closed the file as a missing person's case.

The mother was still searching for her son's dead body, after all these years. There are many mothers like her everywhere. That death could not have been accidental. There was definitely some foul play. Regardless of everything, the mother was still waiting to catch a glimpse of her son's body! We should never turn our eyes away from such sights. I have a notebook with the details of all the corpses I have collected in my life. But I could not find anything about that mother's son.

I have handled almost 1,500 dead bodies until now. In the police station, under the Section 174 of the Criminal Procedure Code (CrPC), one can get the details.*

I have specific information about all the orphaned corpses that I have handled. If anyone comes to me, I should be able to help them. I remember every one of those stranded bodies. Many may have had families. But when their relatives do not want the bodies, they give me a No Objection Certificate saying 'Handed over to Vinu'. I conduct the rites of death.

I spend my own money to give a decent funeral to all the forsaken corpses. In case, the family has to travel from afar, I rent a freezer and ensure the cadaver is kept safely. If someone comes, I hand over the body. Else, I do the final rituals myself. At one stage, I had rented a house just to store the dead bodies.

I know someone who has generously donated his land for conducting the funerals of the abandoned

---

* Section 174 of the CrPC, 1973 details the police's duty to investigate and report on accidental deaths, including suicides. It has now been replaced by Sec. 174 of the Bharatiya Nagarik Suraksha Sanhita, 2023.

bodies; he wishes to remain anonymous. My life has been graced by the pristine goodness of rare human beings who extended welcoming arms of consolation and kindness towards me. This happened when the rest of society rejected me and savagely drove me away. Along with the masters, the graveyard and the corpses I have handled, there are others who have been helping me endure. If not for them, I would have fallen into the abyss long back.

10

The Solitary Man's Army

I shall testify to two truths of my life. One, the eternal truth called death. Second, the solidness of Kerala Police. The khaki-clad humans publicly held me close to their hearts even when the society rebuffed me.

The police station is like my own home. I can enter in any clothes and at any time. I can approach anybody without fear. When I return after collecting a corpse, nobody has ever shouted at me saying, 'You stink, get lost!' If I am hungry, they sense it immediately. They ensure that I am given food. They really care about me. The policemen know when I am upset.

Earlier, if there was no rice in my home, the police would send a sack full of rice at night. There is a shop run by an Ikka, an elderly Muslim man, at Aluva market. The police officers contributed money and entrusted Ikka with that cash. It was to ensure that I never went hungry. This was the way it continued until my wedding.

Even today, the cops buy me shirts to wear. They buy me phones. The object that often goes missing during my work is my mobile phone. On seeing a floating corpse, I dive into the river. I sometimes forget to check if I am carrying a phone. I have lost umpteen phones in the river. What I am using now is the fifth mobile of the year. The moment I lose one, the police officers buy me the latest model. I have actually lost count of the number of mobiles they have gifted me. All the SIMS are in the names of cops. I have had their wholehearted support since the day I started my chosen work.

I am afraid of talking to people. I worry that they would find me irritating. Experiences have sort of hardened that dread inside me. But I am fearless when speaking to the police. If someone in khaki is next to me, I feel emboldened and confident.

Typically, the officers purchase the post-mortem kit and all the material required for conducting the funerals of the corpses when they can. If I need diesel, the cops are there to help. No police officer has ever behaved unpleasantly with me. Neither IPS officers nor the others. I am free to confess all my problems to them. I am allowed to enter the homes and offices of IPS officers. They have served me food, very affectionately, many times.

The media reports are the reason why people recognize me today. In newspapers, on TV and online, there have been reports about my work. The police force played the main role in that. Before the news stories about me started coming in, I was subjected to severe humiliation and rejection. I would unhesitatingly get on with my work, regardless of the state of the corpse. I cannot blame anyone for loathing me, considering the condition of the dead bodies: maggot-ridden, decayed, with exposed flesh and bones ... I do not use any mechanical method for bringing down a hanging body. I embrace the corpse and gently bring it down. It is very important that we should never show disrespect to a dead person. Today, I am no longer surprised that society reviles the one who gathers stinking corpses, crawling with maggots.

Now I can speak about it indifferently, but this was not always the case. When my near and dear, friends and family had abandoned me and I was on the verge of a collapse, the police force presented my case before the media. It was the final, desperate attempt to give me a new lease of life. Their mission was fruitful. The world came to know about someone like me. I started going to work without covering my face after the media reports. It has been three or four years since the media first highlighted my work.

⁂

I was given an award once for saving someone's life. It was the first award I got in my life. The police contributed to the kitty to celebrate that event, giving me an award and a testimonial.

The story of my bravery has comic touches.

I got a call one day. 'Vinu, there is a corpse … case of drowning.'

Reaching the accident spot, I dove into the river. The body was floating at a distance. When I touched it, I realized the man was alive! The body was warm, whereas a cadaver will always be ice cold. I got him ashore safely and took him to a private hospital in Aluva in the ambulance. They admitted the patient. When the man recovered, the hospital billed him ₹6,000. The man ran away from the hospital without paying up.

The police had given the news about my rescue mission to the media. The person I had saved got my details from the newspaper. He called me and abused me in the filthiest language possible! He had set out to kill himself out of poverty. I had saved him and now he owed an additional ₹6,000 that he had to pay! No wonder the poor fellow cursed me.

The hospital management had tried to thrust the bill on me too. With that sort of money, I could have conducted the funeral rites of two abandoned corpses.

I have saved only two people from the jaws of death. And both times, I was offered profanity as my reward. One should never expect gratitude from the living. I have mastered this life lesson. The dead shall obey me. Not the living. They shall go their own way.

The police officers had good intentions behind their gesture of highlighting my rescue. They presumed that society would respect me for my work. When I was fifteen, I was congratulated by the police for the very first time. As recounted earlier, I had retrieved the missing arm of an accident victim, a student of St Mary's. Never shall I forget how SI Babu Sir patted me on my shoulder! I used to meet Babu Sir during the course of my work. It was he who gave me ₹500 as my wages. My father's monthly income was less than that. I became friends with all the police personnel at Aluva station. Many got transferred. Even so, there are unforgettable humans like Babu Sir in my life.

The local police are the first to receive information about a dead body. It is their duty to remove the corpse. They are human beings too. Don't they feel loathing and revulsion doing such work? Nobody trains them to collect corpses. Usually, they rely on others to help them with the task. Before I started working in this field, there were homeless people who did this sort of work. The masters, if they were around, would come to the aid of the cops.

It is extremely rare that someone has dedicated himself to corpse collection. Others would get stone drunk before touching a dead body. But I have never touched a lifeless body after drinking any intoxicant. I do not drink liquor or consume drugs. I smoke beedis. It is a habit I picked up from my masters.

Disposing off a corpse entails money. But the police have no special funds for the purpose. The local bodies have the wherewithal for that: either the panchayats or the municipalities. In the case of Aluva, the municipality is responsible for taking care of the dead bodies. But it is always the cops who pay me for my work – they pay from their own pockets. I have seen that the police end up with the duties of other departments. In case they get to hear about a dead body in a river, the police are supposed to inform the fire force and municipality about the incident. The fire force rescues the living. The municipality has to do the needful in the case of a carcass.

Once the corpse is brought to the shore, the police has to conduct the inquest. A policeman shall be assigned to do 'bandobast'* duty. He has to be with the dead body until the post-mortem is over. The local bodies, which have sufficient funds, are supposed to take care of all formalities until the person is identified. Under the law, a budget of nearly ₹5,000 per body is allotted by the municipality. As far as I have seen and know, I believe that they never spend a penny. Neither do they provide manpower nor any funds. The police cannot evade their responsibility like that, can they? So the cops spend money from their own pockets.

The corpse collector needs to be paid his wages. There are no fixed rates for the job. He is paid whatever he demands. Sometimes, it might be a hefty ₹5,000. Over time, the wages of the corpse collector has indeed increased! Else, nobody would come forward to do the work. The manual labourer, doctor, engineer, judge, IPS officer, all have their incomes, don't they?

---

*Bandobast implies the arrangements that the police has to make to handle a particular situation.

After studying a lot and travelling the world, having achieved much in his career, when a man lies dead and crawling with worms, can you deny payment to the person lifting his corpse? If you haggle over a corpse gatherer's payments, he will drench you with cuss words. Corpse handlers usually get stone drunk before doing their job. An extra burden of ₹500 for liquor.

I entered this field at the age of fifteen by choice. The police officers have told me that there is nobody like me in Kerala or in India. As mentioned earlier, from being a helper of the masters, I slowly progressed to working independently. When I need help, I call others. One must pay ₹2,000–3,000 to the helpers. The rates have gone up nowadays, much like other fields of life. While gathering a corpse crushed under a train, helpers are necessary. You have to carry the cadaver on a stretcher for long distances. When someone is alive, many people would be around. But nobody comes forward to help when a body lies shattered to bits. There will be a rabble uploading videos on social media, but not a single man shall step forward to help. Once the corpse is wrapped up in a mattress, the crowd edges closer. That's the way of the world.

Everyone knows that there are public graveyards for burying unknown corpses. But how many are aware that it involves spending money? Nearly ₹4,000 have to be spent to conduct the burial of a dead body. As mentioned earlier, this comes under the jurisdiction and responsibility of the municipality. In the Cochin Bank public graveyard at Aluva, one has to lift the concrete slab covering the burial spots each time and bury the corpses underneath. If the municipality sends someone to do the work, they expect to be paid ₹500 each, along with a litre of liquor. These are salaried employees, but their demands are clear. If they help in lifting the graveyard's slab, the four of them shall ask for ₹2,000 and liquor. 'Do it if you want' is their carefree attitude. I end up spending from my pocket often.

In the twenty-five years of my work, I have handled the dead bodies of policemen as well. Aren't they human too? Policemen have no set work time. They end up doing innumerable tasks. The police force work like slaves and lead very stressful lives, often losing mental balance. I find them filled with frustration. Once, a SI from a station near Aluva hanged himself. I was the one who handled his dead body. I know of many who have had such terrible ends in the police.

There was an officer at Aluva police station – a gem of a man. He lay bedridden, worms eating his body, towards the end. Except for chewing paan, he had no other bad habits. It started with an ulcer on his leg. Soon, the disease spread to both legs. Nobody, not even family or neighbours approached him. It was I who would remove the crawling worms from his sickly body.

All our so-called relations and friends vanish when our bodies start decaying. They tolerate us only for a while. Except one's mother, all the rest shall leave. The police officer was healthy and active when the disease struck him. I am not aware of the name of that disease. Some say that he was cursed. What nonsense! He was such a well-behaved man.

Worms were gnawing at his living body. He used to kick me in agony when I removed the worms, one by one. As I squeezed his limbs to force the maggots out, the poor man couldn't bear the pain. I would apply medicine on his wounds and bandage him. Once the effect of the medicines decreased, the maggots would start wriggling again inside his flesh. I was not repelled by that sight. In truth, I felt genuine compassion. The officer was bedridden for more than two years. I used to visit him till the end. After his death, his funeral was conducted in the graveyard at Ambattukadavu, with full police honours.

As I said before, I had to bring down the corpse of an officer who hanged himself. I must have handled five or six such cases of unnatural death. Remember the movie, *Nayattu*? The actor Joju George enacts the role of a policeman who hangs himself. It is based on a real incident. How many people know about the sufferings of a policeman?

There used to be a Madam at Aluva police station before. She was a striking figure: tall and smart.

What courage and confidence! If nobody was there for recovering a drowned body, she would promptly dive into the river! Compared to her work, my contribution has been insignificant. Madam was never frightened by the depth of the water. But we hardly hear stories about such brave officers. No media outlet will publish their chronicles. Everybody shrugs that it is 'part of their duty'. The same Madam once saved my life.

I had reached the riverbank, hearing that a corpse was floating in the river. Many policemen and Madam were present on the spot. On seeing the dead body, I dived in straightway. Soon, I was helplessly floundering against a formidable current. Madam recognized my plight immediately. Swimmers are quick to catch the desperate flailing of those who are about to drown. She dived into the river without much thought. I was on the verge of being carried away by the gushing waters. She quickly swam towards me and pulled me to the shore. And then, Madam returned to retrieve the floating corpse, fighting the current!

I know many good police officers. There are those who donate three-fourths of their salary for good causes. 'My ancestors made a lot of money. I have lots of farmland. Enough to live comfortably,' one officer told me. At the same time, there are policemen who struggle to have a bank balance of ₹50 by the end of the month. The cops spend from their pocket for the dead bodies. 'Vinu, you keep the money,' they would say, when I collected the abandoned bodies.

There was a SI at Aluva who was once trying to get reimbursed for fourteen bills. They related to the expenses involved in burying fourteen dead bodies. The Aluva municipality had to pay ₹5,000 for each case. The total amount came to ₹70,000. The municipality never paid the police officer. Unless the bills are paid in a timely manner, the poor cops would be in trouble, since they have paid for the expenses out of their pocket in the hopes of being reimbursed later.

Once, I bought a post-mortem kit for an abandoned body. I also purchased the plastic sheet, gloves and tape needed for various procedures. The body of the deceased was moved in my ambulance. I ended up bearing all the expenses. The Health Inspector created records that stated he had purchased all these items, and he claimed the money. This happened in front of my own eyes. A government officer, earning a decent salary, was financially exploiting a dead body!

A post-mortem kit costs around ₹2,000 to ₹2,500. The more the requirement of clothes, higher the expenses. If the corpse happens to be decaying, more plastic sheets and clothes would be necessary. If the carcass is crushed, many more things are needed, costing more money. If it is an ordinary dead body, a minimum of ₹1,000 of expenses is entailed for the rites. I end up spending from my own savings. It is next to impossible to get the bills reimbursed.

You will recall that it was the police who gave me the dignified job of an ambulance driver when I was on the verge of giving up, haunted by the degradation heaped on me by society's nicknames: 'Shavamvari' or corpse gatherer, and *Shavamnari*, one who smells like a corpse. The officers contributed their money to help me buy an ambulance in December 2018. But I never made any money from driving my ambulance.

All the dead bodies I collected were orphaned ones. When I could not repay the bank loan, I had to surrender the vehicle.

Later, another ambulance was offered to me. A vehicle was lying unused near the Edappally Thevakkal temple. The temple committee graciously gave it to me, free of cost. The police helped me with ₹30,000 to get it converted into an ambulance. But again, abandoned corpses were shifted in my vehicle. I was spending almost ₹4,000 per dead body. My ambulance did not make profits. I ended up owing money to the tailoring shop, where I got clothes for the corpses stitched, the police canteen and the graveyard. Finally, I had to give up the second ambulance too.

My older brother died around that time. Since he had grown up in my maternal grandmother's house, I was never attached to him. After his death, my house, where I lived with my parents, was sold due to accumulated debts. When I became a vagabond, with no home or job, the police again came to my help. They helped us get a rented home and provided us with provisions. Often, we discuss only the worst facets of the police force. It is because our focus is only on the negative aspects of others. We tend to listen eagerly to noxious news. When do we try to see anyone's good deeds?

Kerala Police is my greatest support and succour.

11

Cold, Unfeeling Relations

'Please come to Trivandrum. There is a dead body that needs to be retrieved.' The call came a decade ago. A migrant worker had died, trapped inside a gas pipeline in Sreekaryam. A huge company was installing underground pipes in the area. Since the job was dangerous, they had hired highly skilled workers, mostly from other states. Due to an unexpected mud slide, a worker had fallen to his death inside the pipe. The incident happened late in the evening. Very few people were at the site. Nobody knew that a mishap had occurred.

The next day, seeing the shoes of the fallen man, people rushed to the spot. The police and fire force arrived immediately. Though they discovered which pipeline the man was trapped in, it was difficult for them to retrieve the body. Only a lean, slim person could wriggle inside the pipe with the help of a rope. Since there was no gap through which they could manoeuvre an iron hook, a crane could not be used to pull the body up. There was a very low probability of someone surviving a fall inside the narrow pipe, where oxygen supply was absent.

The rescuer had to be of the same body type as the victim. There was no way a larger person could hoist the body on their shoulder and clamber upwards. The Trivandrum Police started searching for someone to undertake the mission. They shared the message on other police groups. That's how the Aluva Police called me. I started for Trivandrum at night and reached the city by morning.

The police officers took me straight to the accident site in Sreekaryam. It was a prohibited area for the public. I reached there at 7.00 a.m., and the next one-and-a-half hours went in preparation. The medical team examined me meticulously. They checked my blood pressure, my heart rate…all of it. I was made to dress in tight pants. This was to ensure that my clothes would not get tangled anywhere. A hard board was fitted against my chest. A special cream was applied from my shoulder to my elbow so that I could slip down smoothly through the narrow pipe. I wore a jacket, with belts binding my waist, stomach, thighs and shoulders. Along with a spare rope for escaping during a crisis, another rope meant for the corpse, a headlight, torch, wireless connector and an emergency whistle, I was lowered into the pipe head first.

The pipeline was sloping in structure. The company had ensured oxygen supply. I was descending into the depths of the pipe, much like a spider. There was somebody, defeated by death, somewhere below. Death was prowling around, eager to grab me too. But I was not afraid. For the first time in my life, I felt proud of my small stature. It was due to my slight build that I had been selected for the mission.

Twenty feet down, by the torch light's glimmer, I saw the dead body. A man, between thirty-five to forty years old, with a physique similar to my own. One of his arms was broken and twisted. I 'locked' the body by hooking the rope over his shoulder. When the corpse was pulled up, the official machinery: tehsildar, police and fire force were present at the scene. The company paid me money for retrieving the labourer's body. The incident stands unique in my memory because I had never done a recovery from a gas pipeline before. It was also the first time that I had travelled so far for work.

I have dived into rivers with whirlpools to retrieve corpses – I continue to, till date. I can hold my breath only for a minute and a half. If the corpse is floating face down, it is very difficult to pull it ashore. If it is floating on its back, it is very easy to tow it to the riverbank. If the body happens to be in a lagoon with strong undercurrents, it will require the efforts of almost four men.

I have handled dead bodies around which there was a media frenzy. One is risking one's own life while doing the job, every time. The police officers stand solidly behind me. That is my lone support. They ensure that I am vaccinated against getting infections from decaying bodies.

Due to my experience over many years, I have understood certain facts about dead bodies. A doctor might need to do laboratory tests before ascertaining the age of the corpse and time of death. I can predict it, more or less precisely, by observing the nose and eyes. I often think that the gift of smell is one which nature has blessed me with abundantly. From the odour, I can accurately assess how long the body has been dead. The cause of death that I surmise turns out correct most of the time. There are instances when after the recovery of the cadaver murder has been suspected.

Once, there was a woman found dead in the Periyar River. Though I tried to pull the cadaver to the shore, the strong current prevented my mission. I had to wait and watch the whole of the next day, before I could bring it to the shore. It was a case of murder. Someone had killed her and tied the body to a rock. Till date, the killer has not been identified.

I have in my shirt's pocket a weapon which no other layman is permitted to use. It's a surgical blade. The police granted me permission to overcome all objections to purchase this blade from surgical supply shops in my locality. I am allowed to move around with the surgical blade, since I am dutybound to help the police with the inquest. I use it for my duties, such as cutting down the rope of a hanged person or cutting away clothing for documentation. If you examine the file related to Section 174 of the CrPC (duties of a police officer and magistrate in cases of unnatural death) at Aluva Police Station, you will encounter the cases where I have helped the police with their inquests. I have been doing this for close to two decades now.

One cannot simply go and unhook a person who is found hanging. First, a photograph of the floor – with all the objects untouched – is taken. There are dedicated photographers who work with the police. As mentioned before, Tomy Chettan works with them at Aluva. A series of measurements are carried out next: the height of the corpse, vis-à-vis the floor; the distance from the knot to the legs; the length and breadth of the room. Fingerprints are taken professionally using a special powder. Only after seeking permission from the police can anyone cut the knot. I do it with the surgical blade.

If the person hadn't hanged himself, and was murdered, visible evidence would be present on the body as well as in the surroundings. I have taken down the bodies of lovers who died by suicide after binding their bodies together. It is different when someone is killed first and then hanged. In the stance of the corpse, the way the rope is knotted, in the position of the arms, there will be noticeable differences.

On the day a much-discussed murder case happened in Perumbavoor, I was called by the police. A young woman had been killed. All her internal organs had been damaged severely. I was helping in an inquest of a child in Aluva when the phone call came. After finishing my duty, I went to Perumbavoor, straight to the mortuary. I did everything possible to help the police, following their instructions.

When a famous serial actress and her lover died by suicide in a flat in Aluva, it caused much hubbub. The death came to people's notice after four days. The floor was flooded with bodily liquids oozing from the decaying corpses when I stepped in. I slipped and fell flat on my face. I use only a pair of gloves and slippers. After work, I immerse my slippers in rubbing alcohol, also known as surgical spirit.

When people get crushed by a train, it is referred to as 'run over'. In my experience, that category is the one where most deaths occur. Every loco pilot cabin of the trains running in Kerala has been given certain numbers to call in case of such a mishap. The visiting card of the NGO Jeevan-Raksha has been given for the stretch from Aluva Muttam to Airport Road. It has my mobile number. Whenever someone gets run over in that area, the loco pilots get in touch with me.

If they cannot call any NGO, the loco pilots inform the Railway Protection Force or the local police station. On getting a call, I immediately get in touch with the police station under whose jurisdiction the run over has occurred. Unless the policemen arrive, nobody should touch the dead body. The corpse can be shifted only after the police gives permission. In the case of shattered body pieces, these have to be collected from the rail tracks on a stretcher. The next stop is the hospital. The police follows with a request for a freezer. It is to help the family identify the dead person. If any victim is found alive, without waiting for anybody's consent, I take him or her to the nearest hospital.

The police personnel types out the details of the unidentified bodies. The news is published in the newspapers. The search for relatives begins at that point. The corpse is kept in the government hospital's freezer. When the family members arrive, their testimony is recorded. The procedure typically lasts an hour. Afterwards, the inquest is conducted. A post-mortem follows the inquest.

If the family claims the body, it is handed over to them. The job of the police does not end even at that stage. They have to send the preserved parts of the dead body for biopsy. The *mahazar* report or the panchnama has to be prepared at the spot of the accident/suicide. This is the same thing as an inquest: a formal record prepared by the police or a magistrate documenting the circumstances of a sudden, suspicious or unnatural death, or the details of a search and evidence collection during an investigation.

I would accompany them for that purpose. I am the witness in all the cases of unidentified corpses found in and around Aluva. My statement is recorded in all these cases. Once the post-mortem report arrives, the case file is closed.

Usually, the police waits for four days for a body to be identified. Sometimes, they are kind enough to wait for a week. Even then, if nobody turns up, they wait until the inquest is over. If the procedure gets over before 4.00 p.m., the post mortem is conducted. Else, it is postponed to the next day. Then an application is moved before the municipal authorities to bury the body in the public graveyard. The police accompany the dead body, else the public becomes agitated.

At least four men are needed to lift the slab of the Cochin Bank public graveyard, as mentioned earlier. There is a concrete slab covering the burial ground. Beneath it are enclosures of mud, vaults or spaces where each body is buried. After uncovering the slab, the body is buried in an enclosure. If the deceased is unidentified, the body is wrapped in plastic sheet for preservation. The plastic helps to preserve the unidentified body in case there is a future forensic examination.

In such cases, the crime number and the date of post-mortem are written on a paper, which is sealed inside a plastic bottle, and kept along with the dead body in the plastic sheet. In certain cases where an unidentified body is cremated – this decision is taken based on religious markers on the dead body – the cremated remains are buried in the same manner: wrapped in a plastic sheet with a bottle containing the case details. The municipal authority ensures the slab is replaced properly after burial. The workers from the municipality dig 2 ft deep pits usually. Along with a helper, I deepen it to 6 ft. It would take nearly 15 to 25 minutes, depending on the texture of the soil. If it is a rocky terrain, the task would be tougher.

Different graveyards have different types of mud. The dead body's clothes and whatever other objects are recovered should be surrendered at the police station. When someone goes missing, all this specific information about the dead bodies – recorded and maintained at the police station – comes in handy to check if the missing person has already been buried. These objects become part of the evidence. The identity marks on the body are recorded and documented. The police have to be alert until the funeral is completed.

There are many who are condemned to loneliness in our society for no fault of theirs. Such people are destined to be scorched by the rail tracks of isolation at different stages of life. Even when they end up crushed by the train called fate, not a single person turns up to claim the body. As mentioned earlier, I take over the corpses forsaken by families and conduct the funeral rituals. I become son and daughter, mother and father, to these dead bodies.

I might have conducted the burials of 750 unidentified bodies till date. All the exact details are in the register kept at the police station. Of the list, in only two instances has someone approached me later, enquiring after their loved one. One was a helpless mother from Goa, who came searching for her daughter's body.

This happened fifteen years ago. During a train journey, a young woman fell to her death on the tracks. Her body was shattered beyond recognition. I was the one who gathered her corpse. Nobody knows if she slipped accidentally or if someone pushed her from the running train. Nobody came looking for her even after many days. When all searches came to nought, I buried her body in the Cochin Bank public graveyard like other unidentified corpses.

All the while, the mother was anxiously waiting for her daughter. Even after weeks and months, no news reached her. The girl must have become another 'missing case' in the list of the Goa police. Yet, the mother waited hopefully. Maybe at some point of time, she gathered the courage to confront the truth of her daughter's death. She started searching through the lists of unidentified bodies in various places. That's how she ended up at Aluva, following the guidance of the Goa police. Six months had passed by then. From the documented details and the photographs, the grieving mother had identified her daughter. When the turbulent waves of emotions calmed, she requested the police: 'I want my child's remains. I want to take her back home.'

The police officers called me. I checked the notebook where I wrote down the details of all the dead bodies I had handled. Tracing the case number, I recovered the girl's relics for the mother. When the plastic sheet was opened, there was only water and a few bones. After the storm and rain in her heart abated, the mother reverently received the remains of her daughter. She took her daughter away to their homeland.

There could be missing daughters and sons, whose loved ones are still searching for them, among the corpses that I have buried. There could be mothers waiting interminably for their return. I pray always that no other mother comes searching for her child again. There exists no greater pain for a woman, than to see the lifeless body of her child. If a mother passes away, the children might forget her easily. But the death of her child haunts a mother forever.

There are many legal complications in retrieving a buried body. But let me first explain the steps involved in burying a dead body. We leave lime and bleaching powder along with the cadaver so that it decomposes faster. In five months' time, the flesh dissolves. As mentioned earlier, one plastic bottle containing a paper slip with the case number is buried with the corpse. When the missing case enquiries begin, we confirm the case number with the help of that bottle. There are many tests, including DNA, nowadays. Only after ensuring all checks can a dead body be handed over to the family.

❧

In a Malayalam film, there is an iconic scene of the actor Jagathy Sreekumar lying on his back, on a mattress, in the middle of the main road! I too have lain like that once. It was during the Covid-19 pandemic. An intriguing time. When the whole world was shut in, I laid down on a mattress in the middle of the Alappuzha bypass main road. My ambulance always has a handwoven mattress which we call *paya*. Since I had a special pass given to me by the police, I could travel anywhere, even in the pandemic. In between cases, I would lie down on the road when there wasn't much traffic. I collected a total of sixteen dead bodies from houses that remained shut during Covid-19.

I could get away without wearing the mandatory mask, owing to the nature of my work. I had permission for that too. The Second-Class Magistrate

Court at Aluva, on the special recommendation of the Police Surgeon, had issued an order allowing me to not wear a mask during my work. Smelling is a very important component of my occupation. Without assessing the cadaver's odour, I wouldn't be able to make out how many days had passed since the death. A different smell is associated with different decaying parts of the human body. When one organ decomposes, the smell is distinctive. I can easily identify that characteristic. Different odours for eyes, legs, liver, brains and eyes. None of the deductions I have made based on my olfactory sense have gone wrong till now.

When the police were busy catching maskless travellers, people would point at me and ask: 'What about him? He is not wearing one!'

'Do one thing. Take over his job.' That was the police's reply.

To avoid unwanted attention, I started wearing a mask in public.

I have faced much ostracization, humiliation and suffering in my life. But the hurt is more when I see wicked people exploiting corpses for their own selfish ends. There are many like that amid us. When the five-year-old daughter of a migrant worker was cruelly raped and murdered in Aluva, such a manipulation took place.

Usually, when the parents are alive, elaborate funeral rites are not conducted for a dead child as per Hindu tradition. But out of the blue, a religious 'expert' appeared, bragging that he would be conducting the rites for the dead child. Everyone, including the public representatives and locals, fell for his glib words. The man was a big-time fraud who was trying to make the most of the situation. I was the one to gather the body of the tiny child, who had been terribly abused. I was there until the body reached the post-mortem table. The *karmi* was nowhere to be seen until then. Suddenly, he made a dramatic appearance, as if doing a big favour to everyone. But his true colours were exposed rather fast. What should we call such people who do not hesitate even to exploit dead bodies for their vested interests?

I habitually apply the kalabha kuri on my forehead, after my daily bath. There are two reasons why I continue with that childhood custom.

One, it is a part of my identity. For illustration, if someone asks 'Vinu…? Who?', the reply would be: 'The Vinu who applies the kalabha kuri.' It is made by mixing sandalwood paste with many other ingredients like saffron, musk, vetiver and oud.

Second, it has vital indications about my work. If I am wearing the kalabha kuri, it means that I have just taken a bath. While working, the smear of sacred paste gets removed from my forehead. I insist that nobody should touch me knowingly or unknowingly then. Since I deal with corpses, there could be harmful microbes on my body. No person should get infected because of me.

Some people might interpret the mark on my forehead differently. In truth, it has no religious or caste significance. It is just a part of my identity, that's all. My father had the same habit. I started applying the sacred mark at the age of six. By the way, I do not visit temples or other places of worship. Nobody lets me enter such places either. Everybody gets perturbed if I am seen around such sacred spots.

I have been to the temple only once after choosing my occupation.

If someone asks me if I am a believer, this would be my answer: 'Yes, I am a believer. I have faith in the greatest truth I have seen in my life. It is nothing but death.'

12

A Jumble of Nicknames

There are certain tight-fisted, grasping men. Even when facing death, these stingy cheapskates do not let go of their covetousness. They grab whatever they can from anyone. Their hearts are hard as flint, even when a man at the end of his tether begs for help. Society is a simulacrum of that image. It shall beg and plead, clutch, grab and thrive like a weed, and turn into a treacherous Shylock when it is time to give. Eventually, it shall seize ten times the value of what was loaned when it is time to take.

Even before bitter experiences came my way, I had witnessed the true colours of society in the case of the asanmar, my masters. Not only did society pretend not to have seen them, but also brutally drove them from sight. But it couldn't do without the service provided by them. This conceited society, which sprays perfume and struts around boastfully, would have been stinking if not for those like my masters.

Haven't we heard the phrase, 'Truth is stranger than fiction?' The lives of my masters would testify to its truth. They had families, children. They were cast out of their homes for various reasons. These men, from different religions, assembled at Aluva. The masters stayed at railway stations or under overbridges. As far as I am concerned, their work belongs to the purest category. Most of my life's perspectives are their gifts to me. They are my mentors in every sense.

There were eight masters in total. Nobody, leave alone me, is privy to their personal details. They disliked anybody probing too much about their lives. I don't know the real names of all of them. The police used to call them by their nicknames.

Kottody (a favourite local drink), Pambu (a snake; he slithered around like one when stone-drunk; his real name was Velayudhan), Gundu Shivan (he used to sell firecrackers once), Thomas, Parikunju (the oldest of the lot), Antony, South Jose (he usually camped at Ernakulam South) and

Vettoor (that's the name of the place he came from). It was Parikunju who brought them all to Aluva, his homeland.

Parikunju or Parid Ikka, also had a family once, like the rest of the masters. He had been married and lived in Malappuram. After his home life went for a toss, he pitched a tent next to a canal. Later, he shifted to the vicinity of the railway station. One master hailed from Tamil Nadu. South Jose was an expert in arranging for toddy, women and rooms for visitors disembarking at the Ernakulam South Railway Station.

As we have seen earlier, the masters never stayed put at a location. Most of them had criminal cases against them. Some had been to jail. They were ostracized by society and were not friendly. Shopkeepers chased them away, if they requested for a glass of water. From the beginning, I felt a deep respect for them. There was something unusual about these men who did the job that nobody else dared to. After my first two encounters with them, I started addressing each of them as *asan*. Asan means guru, master, mentor or teacher. It is a common way of addressing one's teachers.

As I revealed earlier, it was while retrieving my friend Mithun's dead body that I had seen the masters for the first time. This was not an occupation which they had willingly chosen. Typically, the police forced vagabonds who slept under bridges or at the railway stations to pick up the dead bodies. That's how these men ended up collecting corpses. After a while, the masters adapted themselves to the job. They were not always paid for their hard work. The cops gave them whatever they could afford. The municipality turned a blind eye to their efforts. I was filled with awe and admiration for the unique nature of their occupation and the element of adventure involved.

For the masters, *annam* and *paneeyam* (food and drink) meant one and the same thing. Liquor was their sole sustenance. Local or foreign, arrack or toddy – it made no difference. They ate no other food in the morning. Each went his separate way. After a few hours, the men returned to the original spot. Some would have cash with them. Then they would again get tipsy. Lunch would be shared together. I have never seen them have a cup of tea. They would doze off when the sun was hot. The evening's liquor would arrive in a two litre container. If someone called in between to collect corpses, three of them would leave immediately. 'If there is a need, we shall call you fellows,' they would tell the rest. Whenever the second batch left, I would tag along with them.

Whenever I was with them, they would give me a portion of their food. They ate from the same plate. As I have recounted earlier, I have never seen them wash their hands. Typically, they would sleep after lunch. There would be episodes of storytelling and playing cards.

By dusk, the men would move away once again. The master called Shivan would go fishing in the river. He would sell his catch in Aluva market and purchase toddy. Nobody had a clue where the rest went and what they did. But when the masters re-assembled, they would have a hundred odd rupees with them. The night's quota of liquor would be bought with that money. Soon, they would all be drunk to the hilt. The spate of abuses would begin. It was amusing to listen to these drunken cuss words. Total comedy.

If anyone tried to advise or interfere – regardless of the person being a cop, prominent social activist or moral preacher – the masters would rail fiercely: 'Advice, gossip, confession, backbiting, bitching… don't even start!'

They would gesticulate in a peculiar manner, using the thumb and little finger, while spitting out their angst. It took me a long time to decipher what they were saying exactly.

The men would then start singing. All of them sang folk songs. They all liked the late actor Kalabhavan Mani's songs. They would tap a rock against the rail tracks, to maintain the rhythm. The trains would come whistling by to keep tune to these wild songs. My heart would be in my mouth, even after the last bogey had passed us by. Kalabhavan Mani Chettan, who had long vanished into the depths of darkness, would continue to sing for me, in my masters' voices.

I am denied entry at public functions. To sit in a festival ground or chat with friends and sing with them, are all dreams which are forbidden to someone like me. For me, listening to my masters singing was wonderful. Who else was there to feed me lovingly, tell stories and sing songs? When everyone was inebriated, I would ask: 'Asan, how come you behave like this?'

Their speech slurring, the masters would reply: 'What do you mean? One will fall flat and die tomorrow. What's the point of doing anything?'

They would befuddle me with such philosophy. Jose Asan would forget the world when dead drunk. He would start shouting profanities. But whatever was last night's racket would be forgotten after a night's sleep. They held no grudges against anybody. The masters would sit around in a circle while drinking. Three or four bottles would get over soon. Then the usual ruckus began: expletives, stories, throwing slippers and such like. After getting drunk, only swear words and blasphemies would emerge from their tongues. There might even be pushing and shoving and some pummelling too! But whatever they did, they never misbehaved with me. All of them showered me with affection. I would simply sit at a distance, watching silently.

Some 'decent fellows' of society started complaining about them. The cops would take the masters to the station. It was funny to watch. Since the masters were tipsy, they would plead with the cops: 'Sir, please give us some beedi.' Naturally, they could not drink at the station. Instead, they smoked to their heart's content. By then, the masters would all have become friends again, forgetting the earlier fracas. Some would search for places to urinate inside the station. Fed up, the cops would ask them to get lost!

❧

The masters slept beneath the overbridge or by the side of the railway tracks. One base board, a piece of cloth, a bundle or a sack were their lone possessions. In the morning, they would tuck away their stuff inside some thickets. They would diligently gather all the discarded material around and deposit it in the waste bins. Not a single beedi, piece of plastic or cigarette would be lying around their sleeping space. They did their ablutions at the river side. They bathed once a week.

None of my masters chased after women. I never noticed lusty or randy behaviour from any of them.

Many sex workers would loiter around the area. The masters were friendly with them. But never did they touch a woman or speak a bad word. These men were absolutely decent in that respect.

The masters would often tell me: 'A woman! Hack her apart, you get few pieces.'

A truth which they observed daily at the post-mortem table. Few deep incisions which exposed the skull, the brain, the chest and inner organs. That was all. Whether it was man or woman.

The masters used to help the police surgeon with the post-mortem. In their time, they used weapons like a hammer, sickle, bill hook and chisel to cut open the cadaver.

In the eyes of my masters, all the men in the world were living only for three things: land, women and money. All the wars in the world were fought over these three subjects. Their views on this were crystal clear.

Land or soil: Today or tomorrow, you will need some soil to fall flat on and die.

Woman: Hack her, you get few pieces.

Money: To eat, shit and wipe.

These were the lessons the masters learnt from the much-toasted life. Tell me, can life be defined in a simpler way? The masters were impassive by nature. They displayed no affection or compassion towards anybody. Never would they ask about a dead body's antecedents. On hearing about a death, they would say: 'Some moron could not help hanging himself. Let's go get him.' or 'A family killed themselves drinking poison. Time to go.'

Weren't they cast out by society? They owed nothing to anyone. Even if one among them died, the reaction would be apathetic: 'Here's a corpse.'

On the days they had to collect dead bodies, they would wash themselves in the river after the act. Their weekly bathing ritual at the river was a riotous affair. The masters would swim luxuriantly back and forth for quite a distance. During their swim, if they saw a goat or cow, they would silently steal the animal. Soon, it would be butchered. The sex workers would help them cook the meat. They would eat some of it and sell the rest. It was fun to watch them slice a banana leaf and gobble up huge fistfuls of food off it. They lived in the present. Facing whatever came their way, using the money they had.

Seeing me nibble at my food, the masters would tease: 'Are you feeding an ant, son?' They never forced me to drink or smoke. I have never touched liquor. Nobody drinks in my family. The masters were glad that they didn't have to share their arrack with me! If I took a beedi from their pack and smoked it, they were indifferent. That's one habit I picked from them.

Ever since I have known them, the masters were condemned to live in the streets. They faced abject rejection all their lives. Even food parcels were purchased only from two places. No hotel would entertain them. My masters were delighted that I had chosen this occupation. I ensured they had food every day when they were bedridden in their old age. 'It is a great thing that you are doing. You shall receive blessings for it,' they told me.

Eventually, I started handling extremely decomposed corpses, which they had never seen. There was no question of a re-post-mortem in their time. Never would a buried body be exhumed. But I have dug out a corpse six months after burying it.

Every one of the masters died after vomiting blood. It is the curse of this occupation. Perhaps it is caused by infection from the dead bodies. The police have ensured that I do not suffer the same fate by getting me vaccinated, as mentioned earlier. Mortuary workers and corpse handlers are vaccinated against Hepatitis B, TB and various gastrointestinal infections.

All the masters died after reaching old age. When I met them first, they were nearly sixty. I collected three of their dead bodies from the streets. One master was admitted to Aluva Government Hospital and then shifted to Ernakulam Taluk hospital where he died. I brought his dead body back to Aluva and conducted the funeral. Parid Ikka was injured in a vehicle accident in front of Aluva railway station. He lay paralyzed for a long time. All the masters were laid to rest in the same place: Cochin Bank public graveyard. I ended up burying my masters.

Parid Ikka's relatives arrived only because the police informed them of his death. However, they refused to take his body. When Sivan Asan died at the bus station, his son came because the police threatened him with a case. He, too, rejected his father's body. The police gave Sivan Asan's clothes to his son. I was present at the station. I followed Asan's son when he went away. At Aluva bridge, the young man got down from his vehicle. After warily looking around, he hurled his father's clothes – which he had been holding with repugnance – into the river. A few soiled currency notes were tucked inside the master's shirt. I watched with my own eyes as the son loathingly threw away the last memories of his own father.

These men are living for some profit motives of their own. 'Father' means nothing to them. The police traced Velayudhan Asan's children too. They also washed their hands off their father's dead body. All of the masters had family and relatives. But nobody took their dead bodies.

Thus ended their lives.

The masters lived in a parallel world, an invisible one. Such a world exists in railway and bus stations even today. Busy with the rat race, nobody sees that world. I learnt my work by accompanying the masters, and also many valuable lessons. They were the ones who removed the desire for money from my heart. I had loved a girl once. I wished to marry her, get a good job, make lots of money. Those were my dreams until I met the masters. Afterwards, my life underwent a radical change. My masters had nothing to bless me with, except their insights. Today, if I yearn for nothing in life, it is because of their teachings.

They would philosophize: 'Look around you. Everybody is running so desperately. The corpse which we handled yesterday, he too was busy running about. When that race ended, he reached our hands. Everybody shall die one day. Strangers like us shall remain to run with the dead body. Not a single friend or relative will bother to do it.'

The masters denigrated politicians. But they vouched undying loyalty to the police, who not only respected them but also provided their daily bread. They came from somewhere, and went away somewhere. What they left behind on earth continues through me.

13

Isles of Goodness

This happened quite a while ago, in 2017. An Ikka runs a hotel near Zeenat Theatre in Aluva. The policemen used to have their lunch there. One day, famished, I reached the hotel. Since I used to be chased away from most places, I used to ask permission before entering anywhere.

'Ikka, can I have some rice please?' I asked.

'Yes, come inside.' Ikka replied.

Ikka served me rice and sambhar. Then he asked me if I would like some fish gravy. I agreed happily. As I was eating the meal, a *vakil* (advocate) from a nearby office came in with two clients. I was seated at a corner of the hotel. Even so, the vakil saw me. Ignoring the fact that many people were having lunch inside the hotel, he raised his voice at Ikka.

'You dare to allow fellows like him at a place where dignified people come to have food? Do you know what he does? Gathers rotten, stinking, shattered bodies … Now, he has lurched into the hotel without taking a bath!'

I got up instantly.

Ikka stepped down from the cash counter. 'You sit down and have your meal.'

Ikka forcibly made me take my seat again. Then he turned to the vakil: 'He will have his lunch at my hotel. Sir, I don't care whether you eat here or not. I lose nothing if dignified people like you shun my hotel. I will survive without that money.'

Tears started flowing from my eyes. 'Ikka, I shall leave.' I pleaded.

'You sit there now!' Ikka came near me. He gently grasped my shoulder and served me more rice.

Though my heart and stomach were filled, Ikka went on serving me food. I started sobbing.

'Will show you!' The vakil threatened Ikka and left the place in a huff.

Ikka knew all about me and my occupation. He had often seen me accompanying police officers. The cops had told him everything. Had I known he knew who I was and what I did, I wouldn't have had the courage to enter his hotel. I was overwhelmed with joy and pride that day. Ikka's hotel is the only hotel where I have my meals. He calls me whenever he sees me on the road. Even if no other guest is there, he prepares food specially for me. He is kind and generous.

In society's eyes, across the ages, my occupation has held very low worth. In old films, one sees kings killing the corpse-handlers once the work is over. These murders were stopped in 1953, if my information is correct. I can't be sure of the facts. The authorities used to sentence the poor men to death, terrified that they would infect others with deadly diseases.

One day, I stepped inside a hotel near Aluva Railway Station, along with the police officers. The officers ordered biriyani.

The hotel owners said: 'There's enough biriyani for all of you. Not for him.'

'Why?' The cops asked.

'No rice.'

I understood how matters stood. Seeing my discomfiture, the cops left without having food. They purchased food parcels from another place. We shared the meals at the police station.

That day in 2017, the policemen held a meeting in the Circle Inspector's room. 'Vinu needs a normal life. Shall we give him an award? Let the public get to know about his noble work. We can also buy him an ambulance for a livelihood.'

I have already mentioned this ambulance before; this was the second one that the police had got for me. The police officers pooled in their money and bought me an ambulance. Soon, people started gossiping about my vehicle: 'He must have stolen the money. Vinu is a criminal, isn't he?'

Once, the officer Madam at the police station told me: 'Vinu, every job has its price. Insist on payment. Who deserves it, if not you?'

It was for the first time that someone was guiding me about the value of my work. That too, a police officer whom I respected deeply. After my wedding, when my responsibilities increased, I started asking for payment. I used to get ₹500 till then. Madam's words inspired me and made me proud about my job. She was the woman who rescued me when the river was carrying me away! One of the boldest women that I had ever met in my life. I owe her so much!

An incident occurred four to five years ago.

The Muslim community was supposed to have a big function at Aluva. A leader, busy with collecting funds for the event, was crossing the railway tracks in the evening. He suffered a heart attack and fell on the rails. A train ran over him soon after. His body shattered and many parts fell into the gutter. Informed about this by the authorities, I immediately reached the spot. I stepped into the sewerage, where faecal remains were flowing, and gathered his corpse. Collecting all the splintered body parts, I went to the hospital.

The leader's son and relatives were waiting for us. The police officers pointed to me and told the man's son: 'This young man collected your father's corpse.' The man did not respond; he was in shock at his father's unexpected demise. The mortuary was overflowing with people.

Whenever I collect a dead body, I search for anything that might help us identify the deceased. That day, I recovered nearly ₹2 lakh from the leader's pocket. I handed over the amount to the man's son via the police officers.

After the post-mortem, the cadaver was shifted to the mosque for the final rituals in my ambulance. When I was trying to help them bring down the body, some men snapped angrily at me: 'Kaafirs should not touch the dead body!'

These were powerful men holding top positions at the mosque.

Hearing these words, the man's son leapt out of the ambulance. 'Only this Kaafir was there to gather my father's body from the gutter! Vinu removed human feaces from his crushed limbs. None of you should touch my father! I will not have his burial in your mosque! Vinu shall touch my father's body before anyone! Else my father shall never be at peace.'

The young man was enraged. Many people supported him. The elders were on one side and the young men on the opposite. It was the first time that someone had argued for my sake in front of such a massive crowd!

There was a village I never visited, out of fear of my work being exposed before the public. One day, I was asked by the police to help them with a case there. My first wife's village, Vyppinkara. The police arranged for this knowing fully well about my life. It was such a proud moment for me!

Someone had hanged himself at Vyppinkara. The death came to light after three days. There were people available to collect corpses. But the police officers who knew me, insisted that I come all the way from Aluva to make a point. When I reached the place, many people, including antagonistic temple committee members were waiting for me. They had once behaved harshly with me during my divorce.

I embraced the corpse close to my chest and gently took down the body. Else, it would have broken into bits. That was the pitiable condition of the dead body. There were many who praised me that day in the village.

~

As mentioned earlier, when I was left disconsolate, without a home or vehicle, the police officers arranged for a news report about my life in the media. When it was telecast on popular channels like Marunadan Malayali and Flowers, many viewers watched it. Many people started calling me afterwards.

There was an Amma from Canada who called at night. 'Son, I am Anathalakshmy Nair, almost seventy-six years old. I am leading a retired life in Canada. My children are not with me. Vinu, you must be my grandson's age. Call me Amma.'

Another day, Amma called and said, 'You should go to Thodupuzha today.'

'Why, Amma?'

'Reach there first.'

Amma gave me the details of the place and the person I was supposed to meet. When I went to Thodupuzha, there was a tempo traveller which had run 30,000 km and been converted into a hearse van for transporting dead bodies. It was a gift for me.

Amma called again and asked me to visit another place. This time, it was a Maruti Omni ambulance! Due to the kindness of that affectionate Amma, I became the owner of two ambulances.

Amma keeps calling me and talks with great affection. Once she asked me what else I wanted. I pleaded that I wasn't in need of anything. But she did not listen. A freezer for storing corpses and a generator were purchased for me. She also sent me money.

Another day, she sent home a water-ambulance costing ₹1,65,000. It is a motorized boat which is used while scouring for corpses in rivers. That Amma, whom I have not seen till now, has spent more than ₹5 lakh for my sake. Amma uses internet calls. No video calls, just voice.

I yearn to see Amma with my eyes. But that wish will not come true. 'Son, I shall stay in Canada till I die. Humans remain human only because some wishes do not come true.'

The destiny of some people is to help others. Amma's life is one of that kind. She embodies pure goodness. Never have I known anyone else like her. She sends messages occasionally. I have no idea how I am supposed to pay back all that affection.

Imagine a frail man, with a trembling body and wounded mind, struggling to make his way over a dangerous bog. I was in such a state for many years. The earth was likely to slip from under my feet at any moment. Humiliation was piled steep on my head. Yet, I walked on. My aim was to reach the yet unseen bodies, bereft of life, patiently waiting for me. The great power – God, Time, Fate, Nature or whatever name it is referred to – must have felt compassion for me. It offered me many gifts I could hardly dream of! The most precious of those are with me today – my second wife and second child.

The stranger, a young lady, stepped into my life most unexpectedly. It happened a few years ago, in 2021. I was working as an ambulance driver at Jeevan Raksha Trust in Aluva. Bincy worked as a nursing assistant at the Trust. Her house was in Nedumbassery, near Cochin International Airport.

While chatting with other colleagues at the office, I used to speak to Bincy too.

One day, when I was shifting a patient to palliative care, Bincy accompanied me. Usually when a woman patient is being transported, a female nursing assistant comes along. That day, we talked for a long time. Perhaps, it was for the first time in years that I was conversing with a living woman!

Occasionally, Bincy continued to travel with me in the ambulance. We became good friends. One afternoon, after hospitalizing a patient, we saw a bike lying toppled on the main road. I jumped out without much forethought. Bincy stepped down after me. Her goal was the same as mine. Together, we lifted the injured man into the ambulance and drove straight to a hospital. It was late by the time we left the hospital.

I drove unhurriedly through the desolate roads. We were in the Omni ambulance. Bincy was seated to my left. Though her gaze was fixed on the road, I felt that her mind was elsewhere. I presumed I was imagining it, since my mind was wandering too. It was a dream come true – or rather, beyond any dream – that I was driving through the enchanting darkness, with a girl next to me.

We chatted for a while before lapsing into a long silence. It was then that Bincy opened up her heart. 'I like you, Vinu Chetta.'

A sudden fever seized my body! I don't know if I pressed the accelerator or the brake in that moment.

'What was that?' I asked, not believing my own ears.

'I like you, Vinu Chetta.'

My brain harshly pushed away everything surging within ecstatically, and snarled at me: *She's joking!* There could be no other explanation. Here was a girl more educated than me, who had a higher status in society, financial and otherwise. An only daughter of her parents, she came from a reputed family, following a different religion. Bincy was hardly twenty-two years old. I was a thirty-five-year-old man, who had failed in the tenth standard. I had also been married once and had fathered a child.

'Bincy, are you serious?'

'Yes.'

The power called Time had made a young woman, an acquaintance of a few days, say those precious words – words I had once yearned to hear from the lips of a girl at school. A young woman, whom I never deserved, was telling me that she liked me!

I started perspiring in the cold November night. Hiding the tsunami-like emotions that were welling up inside my heart, I spoke dryly: 'I have no time to act like a fool in love. My circumstances are very different.'

'I know your circumstances. I want to marry you.' In a moment, Bincy transformed from a naïve girl into a mature woman. Her words were firm. Seated next to me, near my heart, was a young woman whom I could never have even dreamed about! A proposal for marriage, which I thought was next to impossible in my life. All my accursed yesterdays, unknown to her, creating a distance between us, vanished in a moment. Seated in the front of that Omni ambulance, Bincy and I dreamt of a new life that night.

Bincy had watched the media reports about me many times. She had noticed me when I collected corpses near the railway crossing in her neighbourhood. She had revealed her wish to marry me while being fully aware of my life. She admired my work, something that nobody else dared to do. It was the most beautiful night of my life.

Things happened very fast afterwards. I could not imagine visiting Bincy's house with a marriage proposal. So we decided to get our marriage registered officially. When the police officers got to know about it, they came forward to help. 'We are there with you. Go ahead, Vinu.'

In March 2022, Bincy and I got our marriage registered at the Sub Registrar's office at Aluva. One month went by, without us disclosing the news to anybody other than our well-wishers in the police. A formal wedding ceremony, attended by my parents, close colleagues who help me from time to time and a few people from the police department, was solemnized on 25 April. Then we moved to my rented house in Aluva.

When we called Bincy's family to inform them about our marriage, two cars filled with agitated relatives came rushing to our place. It was terrifying. I was sure that they would hack me to bits. But the police officers ensured my protection. Bincy boldly told her family that she had willingly married me and wished to live with me. They went back wordlessly.

Though many relatives called to warn her that a life with me would be hellish, Bincy ignored them. One day, a friend of Bincy's asked her: 'Aren't you ashamed to live with this Shavamnari, a corpse-stinker?'

'That's my decision. Don't interfere in my life!' Bincy cut the call ruthlessly. She blocked the so-called 'friend'.

Today, we have another blessing in our life. Little Varshit, who runs around merrily in our home. When we went for a checkup at the Aluva Hospital after Bincy's delivery, an old Muslim woman, an Ittha, talked to my wife very lovingly. Apparently, she had watched the news about me. 'God will bless you dear, for giving a life to someone doing such sacred work!'

Though Bincy lost many friends after marrying me, many new people came into our lives, having heard about us through media reports. Some started calling her on her phone. Many expressed respect and appreciation for my work.

These are wonderful things for someone like

me, used to degradations and harsh treatment all his life. Bincy wishes to become my companion at work, after our child grows up a bit. Finally, I have someone who loves me unconditionally, while knowing everything about my life. She stands by me, in both tears and laughter. My wife, and the son she gifted me with, are my greatest strengths today.

Bincy is the most pristine star, bestowed by Time, for someone desperate for a refuge in the endless darkness.

14

An Extraordinary Dream

Is there anyone alive who does not have a dream? Everyone is racing after theirs. Whatever be the dreams, irrespective of the heights we fly, regardless of everything we achieve, all human beings end up in the same place. Soil. Six feet of soil. That's all the land that a man needs. I believe that soil is the birthright of everyone fated to live and die on this earth.

I have found an answer to the questions 'Who am I?' and 'Why am I alive?' in my inconsequential life. I want to create a graveyard of my own. That's my destiny. That is also my dream.

Even when I say, 'my own', it does not belong to me. The graveyard belongs to whoever rests there. I shall be the caretaker of that soil. Any human or animal can come there as a corpse and rest forever.

I have nothing to call my own. I am indebted to many. Even today, I have no house of my own. But more than a home, I dream of owning a graveyard. Maybe you might ask, 'Isn't it a man's duty to fulfil a householder's responsibilities?' I am working hard to take care of my parents, wife and child. So long as the Kerala Police exists, my family shall have a refuge. My belief is unshakable and my life is a testimonial to my trust.

Bincy often laughs and says, 'I have experienced much sweetness of life. I wished to taste some bitterness. That's why I decided to live with you.' The journey towards my dream becomes easier with a partner like her. She shares my dream. Bincy has added some embellishments to it. A graveyard full of flowers and sprawling trees. If we build a house for ourselves, it shall fall to ruin after we die. But a graveyard shall thrive across time.

During the great flood of 2018, many people came forward to do my life's work. When rescue operators were competing with one another to pull out lifeless bodies of humans, I was searching for carcasses of animals. As few of us travelled in a boat, under the railway tunnel, we saw a buffalo's carcass. Diving into the depths, I brought ashore that dead animal. I buried many animals during those difficult times. There was none to take care of the poor cattle that had drowned.

When I do the rounds of the river, I encounter sacks filled with animal carcasses. That's also murder, isn't it? These creatures were drowned in the waters in sacks. We ignore these incidents because these are not human bodies. Man and the gods he made never bother about animals.

People chase after anything with value. If you have anything valuable, there will be someone to claim it. Human beings are always calculating 'what's in it for them'. Nobody seems to realize that it shall all end in the soil.

There are billionaires on this earth of ours. When

they die, do they take back anything with them? Our bodies are meant to diffuse into the *panchbhoota* – the five elements of nature – earth, water, fire, air and ether. The moment life leaves the physical body, one is a mere corpse. After death, nobody asks, 'Has the man been shifted to the burial ground?' Instead, they ask, 'When is the corpse's burial?'

We living beings are not cognizant of our inconsequence. Nothing is going to change in nature because of our deaths. In my view, air is the lone, essential entity. The moment it vanishes, life ends too. In the time we spend searching for many things, isn't it better to search for our own selves?

Today, I dream of my own graveyard. There is a reason behind it. The condition of public graveyards is pathetic. The way burials are conducted is even more horrid. Nobody should have to leave like that. As mentioned before, one has to spend almost ₹4,000 to give a decent burial to an orphaned body. The locals help in the case of someone known to them. But what about abandoned bodies? Who shall take responsibility for those? I accept such cadavers.

Whichever public graveyard is open, I try to bury them there. If I can identify the religion of the person, I try to follow the rites of that specific religion, else I follow my heart. But there are many problems. A municipality shall accept in its graveyard only those dead bodies falling under its jurisdiction. Basically, for the dead to return to the soil, they have to follow the rules of the living!

Some years ago, a disabled young man died in a rented house in Aluva. Only his elderly mother lived with him. Her husband had left them a long time ago. The house owner forbade her from burying her son in the compound. Maybe, the man had his own reasons. Where would that poor mother go with her dead son's corpse? Seeing her utter helplessness, the police got in touch with the panchayat. They also called me. I took over the boy's body.

If you have a Letter of Recommendation from a panchayat member on his official letter pad, and a No Objection Certificate from the police, any relative or friend can take over the responsibility of burial of the corpse. But the locals did not come forward to help the mother. When the public burial ground is not available, I have someone whom I call for help. A great man, who has allotted his land at the district border, free of cost, to bury abandoned orphans. I called him that day. With two helpers, I went there at night. In the morning, we conducted the final rites of the body.

Every person born into the world has relatives. Those who are left alone in various circumstances become orphaned bodies. I know well-off men, abandoned by their families, now living near the railway tracks. Once, I saw a poor mother in Chottanikkara. She was living on the streets as a vagabond. At one point in time, she was a very rich woman. The mother registered all her properties in her son's name. After his marriage, she was pushed out of her own house. The mother's life was an illustration of a principle: never be conceited about having children. She wished to go to Kashi and give up her body. But the woman ended up at Chottanikkara Temple. She had matted hair like a yogini and spoke for a long time with me. She told me stories about the *aghoris* of Kashi, who consume the flesh of corpses.

I also remember a father's story. I retrieved his lifeless body at the railway track at Ambattukadavu. I was the one to shift the corpse to the mortuary. When the police took evidence, his son started sobbing inconsolably. The man had fought with his father. In the heat of the moment, he had shouted, 'Get lost!' Unable to tolerate his son's harsh words, the father had decided to get lost from life. What I retrieved from the railway tracks were the remains of a man shattered both in his body and mind.

Two years ago, I had collected the corpse of an old woman. There was a gold chain around her neck. A strong reason for the relatives to flock around the corpse. Till that time the woman had been living on the streets. After her death, all her relatives claimed the gold chain, but not the dead body!

Many people argue over settling the bills of burial. They will even demand a receipt for the ambulance expenditure. Need to keep account of everything, right? It does not matter to them that it is their father or mother lying dead in front of their eyes. Only money is important, even at that juncture!

I have learnt all these lessons from my experiences over decades. I am not greedy for any materialistic pleasures or money. Neither do I have many desires in life. In my view, these are transient. The solitary truth is death. Time is my god. I believe in the circle of time: Kalachakra.

Whatever we do, shall be returned with due interest. No need to wait for the next birth at all. That's how the circle of time works. It is an inseparable part of our own selves. Blood starts pumping from the heart, traverses to each and every organ, and returns to the heart. Consider that as the biggest illustration. Whatever we do shall circle around and finally come back to our own selves. That's for sure.

My parents now live with me, Bincy and our son Varshit. My father's job was ironing the clothes of others. But there was an unambiguous, irremovable crease in his own life. It was Vinu, his son. The guilt that my parents would never have a peaceful life because of me has always persisted in my mind. Due to that feeling, until now, I have never been able to have a meal with them, while conversing openly.

Even if it is just for a day, I want to make my parents happy. I wish to see them genuinely happy. My father is always deep in thought. I still remember going to him for the money to buy the first Bajaj petrol autorickshaw. He was cleaning the huge water tank of Sapna Bar in Aluva, perspiring from head to toe. This was a side job he had taken on for additional income. Acchan has brought me up enduring many sacrifices.

'What do you want to be when you grow up?' My parents would ask me in my childhood.

'Police!'

'No, not a petty cop!'

I still have not understood that response.

The same family members who discouraged me from becoming a policeman stood against my wishes when I grew up. I shall never make my child suffer like that. I will never take a decision for him or disallow what he decides for himself. His life, his wishes.

I believe in souls. Not in ghosts. I have seen ghouls, spectres and sprites – in the form of fire, air and water. They have the power of destruction. You can never trust or mistrust these. Can we live without them? Nature is both our god and devil. Rock, soil, tree ... everything in nature has a sublime life spirit of its own. We should learn to respect them all.

My work involves handling corpses without causing any damage to the organs. Even if I am offered some other work, I cannot accept it. Many people called me after watching the TV channel reports. I was promised money and jobs. I politely refused all of those. One person sent me money, which I returned promptly. A missionary father from Aluva promised me a job in the congregation's Spanish cemetery. I declined that too. The kind Amma from Canada has already given me everything I need. I only want a graveyard now. There are no legal obstructions for achieving that dream. Just a few other challenges. Land, for example. It should ideally be isolated, while having facilities of water supply.

Recently, there were talks of a government job. There is no *sarkari* designation for the work that I do. The municipality has such a job opening, but I am not keen on taking it up. It shall be like imprisoning me at a single place. I won't be able to attend to corpses whenever I am called to help. Instead, I shall be restricted to working in a single municipality. Now I am free. I can devote myself to dead bodies anywhere, unconditionally. I am fully satisfied with my present liberty.

My desire is to respectfully bid farewell to human beings – send the one who emerged from soil, back to the soil. We came alone and shall return alone to the earth. Even if we arrive into light, our return is to the realm of darkness. I wish to shine a light on those travellers, humbly sending people off to rest. That's my life's purpose.

'Someone else will do it. Why are you being so stubborn. Is it *your* job?' That's a question I am asked often.

Any job in this world can be done by someone else. Yet, why does everyone pursue their jobs sincerely? Burying abandoned dead bodies is my occupation, and insisting on some soil for the purpose happens to be my ambition. I am not worried about what others are doing. I should focus on the work before me, shouldn't I?

I used to be a coward who was afraid of darkness. I would avoid stepping on cow manure and get nauseated by anyone sneezing openly. That young boy grew up to become me. I have eaten food while seated next to a decomposing body. I have dealt with blood splattered bread too. I am not repelled by anything now. Time shall not transform someone so drastically without reason – that belief guides me onwards.

I do not fear anything. The biggest dread is death. There is nothing beyond that, is there? And I adore death. It is when I started seeing death at close quarters that all fears about life left me forever. Fear motivates human action today. Fear of God, fear of death, fear of family, fear of life's burdens, fear of fate …

I accept whatever comes my way. All I need is some soil where I shall rest on one day … As my wise masters advised, I foresee only the ending. Life means just that, as of now.

Epilogue

Who can confidently state that when my body lies maggot ridden on a desolate road, someone shall gather me affectionately? Even the most intimate of our relatives and friends might be horrified to take a second look. It is doubtful whether one's parents, siblings, wife or children would be able to stand such a sight. Many might throw up, faint or flee. It is very natural to feel repulsion and horror.

Vinu is not repelled by rotting corpses. He treats them with respect and love. Here is someone who lives amid us, willing to embrace a stranger's decaying body, gather it close to his heart and offer it a dignified burial. It is this assurance that Vinu gives to society. For any land under the sun, a man like Vinu is a rare sight, a highly improbable phenomenon, like a heavenly comet.

The most noble social service is an act of great compassion. Vinu becomes an anchor for all those abandoned dead bodies that are ignored by all. The souls free themselves, leaving behind their lifeless bodies on Vinu's frail shoulders. What words can do justice to the benevolence inside Vinu, the saviour of the forsaken corpses on the streets? Someone who gives them a dignified farewell, burying them in the bowels of the earth? What wondrous words should I use to describe Vinu, who dreams of a graveyard where all orphans have a final resting place?

I am very grateful to this man. It was he who provided the insight that among those sleeping near the rail tracks, under the overbridge and in the foyers of petty shops – along with the homeless and lost, the thieves and pimps – there could be philosophers and saints. Next time, I pass beneath Aluva bridge, my eyes shall go searching for those who sleep there. Not many would have experienced life as deeply as them. Also, not many would have laughed off the heaviness of life so effortlessly and lightly.

As one struggles to roll the boulder of life, to the summit of overarching ambitions, there are those who laugh delightedly at watching it roll back down.

While contemplating that Sisyphean myth, men like Vinu appear like gurus.

Most human beings who have recognized the truth of life are not found sleeping on luxurious silken beds. Instead, they repose beneath overbridges or enjoy the cool shade of the ancient tree named 'Mrityubodham' or the Awareness of Death.

Niyas Kareem

Acknowledgements

This book would not have been possible without the encouragement, expertise and generous support of many individuals. My profound gratitude goes out to:

My father, who introduced me to the magical world of stories and made me realize the power of the written word.

Alwin George, who first brought the inspiring life story of Vinu P to my attention.

Ministhy S., whose brilliant translation and unwavering guidance were instrumental in realizing this English edition.

Parth Mehrotra, my editor, and Krishna Sawant, the assistant copy editor at Juggernaut Books, whose meticulous editing and attention to detail shaped this book into its final form.

Noushad and Sidharth at Mathrubhumi Books for their enduring support.

G. Harikrishnan for his evocative photography; Santhosh Aechikkanam, Sheela Tomy, Benyamin and V.J. James for their generous endorsements; and Zainul Abid, Vinu Joseph and V.N Ramkumar for their creative contributions.

Dr P.B. Gujral, retired police surgeon, for his invaluable time and expertise in clarifying the legal procedures surrounding the investigation of an unnatural death.

A unique acknowledgement is reserved for the Indian Railways; trains provided me with a moving sanctuary and the perfect ambience where most of this book was written.

I thank my Malayalam readers who first embraced Vinu. Their genuine, passionate reviews across multimedia platforms carried this story forward and made it reach a wider audience.

Finally, to my family for being my constant anchor throughout this journey. This book exists because of the space you created for me.

Niyas Kareem